Good Health is Possible!

CONTENTS

Foreword

This book is dedicated to the many thousands of advisers who have passed on the vital information about Cellular Medicine in Germany and other countries. It is our common goal to build up a new health system which finally serves the interest of the people.

This book constitutes the final stroke under a falsely conceived health system. It provides proof that for a hundred years endemic diseases, under the influence of the drugs industry, have artificially been kept alive as global market outlets for what were mostly ineffective and dangerous pharmaceutical treatments.

This book is proof that the most significant "common diseases" of today are not diseases at all but the inevitable consequence of years of deficiency of vitamins and other natural substances whose function is essential to the metabolism of millions of body cells.

This book lays the foundation for heart attacks, strokes, high blood pressure, cardiac insufficiency, diabetic complications and other diseases to become soon a thing of the past soon.

This book is the signpost for any politician to stand up for fundamental reform of the health system. Above all, those untenable laws which form an obstacle to the spreading of this vital information must be eradicated.

This book is also the answer for doctors and other members of the healthcare professions who have recognised the blind alleys of conventional medicine and are opening up new routes. Cellular Medicine is the basis for health provision of the future.

Above all, this book is the answer for hundreds of millions of patients all over the world who for decades were at the mercy of the drugs industry and the blind alleys of outmoded medicine. Here is the answer to their health problems.

We invite you to join us in building of a new health system by broadcasting the information in this book wherever you go. Pass the book on to your friends, acquaintances, colleagues, and neighbours. Take it to your club, church or other occasions. Give it as a birthday present – instead of flowers. Give it to your doctor, or have it displayed in their surgeries.

You will be helping other people and saving lives.
This book was written by patients and those afflicted. It is to them that we owe our thanks. This book is only the beginning, the documentation of the success of Cellular Medicine continues and will one day fill whole shelves. Send us your report for the next edition of this book. You will be helping many people with this.

My thanks also to Mrs Angelika Zuta-Sadovic, Mrs Marian Peters, and Mrs Christina Rauch for the collating and processing of the texts, and in particularly to Mr Dirk Brandt for co-ordinating the compilation of the documentation.

Dr. Matthias Rath MD

INTRODUCTION
Cellular Medicine – a breakthrough in the natural prevention and causal therapy of common diseases

Dr. Rath is considered the founder of Cellular Medicine, the new understanding that most common diseases are based on deficient vitamin supply to millions of body cells. This new concept of health and disease is the basis for the remarkable success stories documented in this book. The scientific principles of Cellular Medicine are summarised below.

The cells in our body perform a multitude of functions: glandular cells produce hormones, white blood corpuscles manufacture antibodies and cardiac muscle cells produce electrical energy for the heart to beat. The specific task of each cell is determined by the genes in the cell nucleus comparable to a metabolism software programme. Although these tasks may be very different, each cell uses the same bio-energy sources (biological catalysts) for a multitude of vital biochemical reactions within the cell. Many of these biological catalysts cannot be produced by the body itself. It must be taken externally as a supplement.

Vitamins, minerals, trace elements and certain amino acids are of particular importance here. The most important of these essential biological catalysts are summarised in Dr. Rath's vitamin programme. Without the regular and optimum supply of these bio-energy sources, functional deficiency of the cells, organ malfunction and subsequently disease are the result.

The constituents of
Dr. Rath's vitamin programme catalyse
thousands of biochemical reactions
In each cell

The most important
Biological catalysts

- Vitamin C
- Vitamin B-1
- Vitamin B-2
- Vitamin B-3
- Vitamin B-4
- Vitamin B-5
- Vitamin B-6
- Vitamin B-12
- Carnitine*
- Coenzyme Q-10
- Minerals
- Trace elements

Single cell

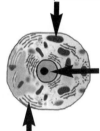

Energy centre
(mitochondrion)

Cell nucleus
(nucleus)

Cell production centre
(endoplasmatic reticulum)

The metabolism software programme in each cell is determined precisely by the genetic information in the cell nucleus.

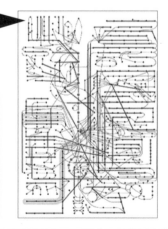

The constituents of Dr. Rath's vitamin programme are used as biological catalysts and bio-energy sources in each cell. They are indispensable for the optimum functioning of millions of cells

Cellular Medicine helps keep heart and circulatory disease in check

Cellular Medicine forms the scientific basis for winning the battle with death from heart disease. The correlations are easy enough to understand. The heart and circulatory system are the mechanically most active organ systems in our body. As a result of the constant pumping action to maintain blood circulation, the cells of the circulation system have a particularly high turnover in cell energy and a particularly high consumption of vitamins and other biological catalysts.

First of all, the most important types of cell making up the heart and circulation system:

- **The cells of the blood vessel walls:** the endothelial cells form the barrier between the bloodstream and blood vessel wall. These cells are also responsible for optimum viscosity of the blood and blood supply. The smooth muscle cells of the vascular wall are responsible for optimum stability and elasticity.

- **The cells of the cardiac muscle:** the principle task of the cardiac muscle cells is to ensure the pumping action of the cardiac muscle. Furthermore, some of the cardiac muscle cells are specialised to produce electrical stimuli for the heart to beat and to convey these stimuli to the tissue of the cardiac muscle.

- **The blood cells (blood corpuscles):** millions of small blood corpuscles circulating in our blood are nothing more than cells. They are responsible for transporting oxygen, for defence and elimination of waste, for the healing of wounds and other functions.

The heart and circulation system is made up of millions of cells

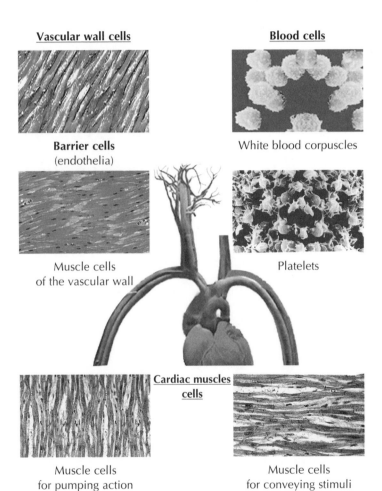

Vascular wall cells

Barrier cells
(endothelia)

Muscle cells
of the vascular wall

Blood cells

White blood corpuscles

Platelets

Cardiac muscles cells

Muscle cells
for pumping action

Muscle cells
for conveying stimuli

Notes

2

- **Heart attack**
- **Stroke**
- **Hardening of the arteries**
- **Circulatory disturbance**

**Dr. Rath's
Cellular Medicine:
programme for natural prevention
and basic theraphy**

The facts about coronary heart disease

Every second European dies as the result of arterial calcification of the coronary arteries (cardiac infarction) or of the carotid arteries and cerebral arteries (stroke). The epidemic proportions of this disease can be attributed to the fact that not enough was known until now about the causes of atherosclerosis.

Conventional orthodox medicine is essentially limited to treating the symptoms of atherosclerotic deposits. Calcium antagonists, beta-blockers, nitrates treatment and other medicines were prescribed to ease problems with angina pectoris. Surgery (by-pass operations and coronary angioplasty) is performed to mechanically improve the blood supply through constricted arteries. None of these conventional therapies attempts to treat the actual cause of the atherosclerosis, the instability of the artery wall.

Cellular Medicine has made a breakthrough in a modern understanding of the cause, prevention and causal therapy of coronary heart disease and other forms of atherosclerotic disease of the heart and circulation. The chief cause of this is chronic deficiency of vitamins and other cell factors in millions of cells of the arterial wall. This leads to instability of the artery wall, numerous lesions, atherosclerotic deposits and resultant from that, heart attack and stroke. The most important measure in preventing heart attacks and strokes is optimum addition of vitamins and other cell factors. The following letters from patients with cardiac insufficiency emphatically confirm this medical breakthrough. Cellular Medicine therefore helps to eradicate this common disease.

Heart attack, stroke, atherosclerosis

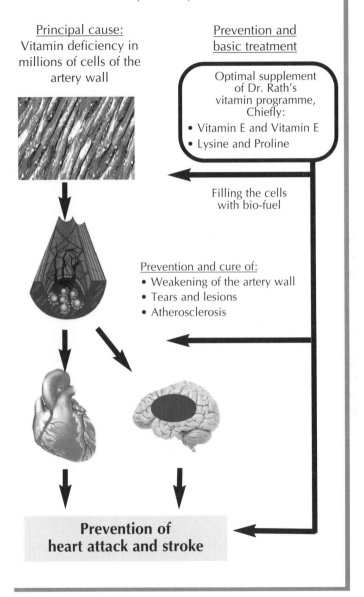

Principal cause:
Vitamin deficiency in
millions of cells of the
artery wall

Prevention and
basic treatment

Optimal supplement
of Dr. Rath's
vitamin programme,
Chiefly:
- Vitamin E and Vitamin E
- Lysine and Proline

Filling the cells
with bio-fuel

Prevention and cure of:
- Weakening of the artery wall
- Tears and lesions
- Atherosclerosis

**Prevention of
heart attack and stroke**

Dear Dr. Rath,

This time last year I had just had an operation after a stroke. I only survived this stroke without further damage because the operation was carried out quickly and by an experienced angioplasty surgeon. Calcareous blockages were removed from both carotid arteries. But what about the calcium in the smaller arteries, in my brain and feet and heart? The senior consultant told me that another operation was not possible and further blocking of the arteries must be prevented.

When I left hospital my son recommended that I accompany him to a lecture to hear something about correct diet and vitamins. We then began taking Dr. Rath's preparations.

This produced the following verifiable results to the astonishment of all the doctors treating me:

- **No new calcification of the carotid arteries was found** but, on the contrary, **decalcification**. These were the findings in May this year at the clinic where I had the operation in July last year.
- I have been diabetic since 1986 and already had **circulatory problems in my legs** and feet. These have **almost disappeared**. No more cold feet. The extremely high **blood sugar level** has considerably been reduced; the level is **normal again** through taking *Diacor* in conjunction with *Vitacor Plus*.

- My **eyes** have improved, the **internal pressure is normal again**.
- Heart complaints, particularly at night, have gone, I can sleep well. Also, my previously diagnosed **arrythmia has gone**. My short-term memory has improved. I can solve normal crossword puzzles, one after the other.
- There has also been a considerable improvement for my wife who has suffered from migraine and painful joints for years. Also her **blood pressure is normal again**.

All in all we have taken on a new lease of life, can deal with our age with much more optimism and are less afraid about the future. For us, a new life has begun. I am 65 years old and feel like 50 again!

Yours sincerely,

W.B.

Dear Dr. Rath,

I am 61 years old and have been suffering from **angina pectoris** for four years – I have obviously inherited the susceptibility from my father. I was plagued and restricted by sudden **shortage of breath** at the slightest exertion. In January last year I had a **by-pass operation**.

I began your basic vitamin programme on 14th June last year and from January this year I have also been taking the supplementary programme *Arteriforte*. After twelve weeks I had no pains any more, not even with increased exertion. **I no longer feel pressure on the heart or breathlessness** – which I still had after the operation! My **blood pressure** has returned to **normal** since December last year, the operation scars have healed well, today there are no pains from the scars at all.

After the last electron radiation tomography at the University Clinic Erlangen-Nürnberg the doctors there diagnosed my condition as follows: "Given the subjective absence of symptoms and good resilience, we can see **no indication of any progression of the coronary heart disease which was present**". – The atherosclerosis which caused me so much trouble has therefore actually been halted.

I feel absolutely fit. The acid test was when I was able to lift 40-kg sacks up to a ladder onto a 10-m high scaffolding.

I am thankful I heard about your therapy. It has saved my life – **and all without any side effects**! I don't need medicines any more now!

Yours sincerely

Werner Wolf

Dear Dr. Rath,

In autumn 1995 my uncle's health deteriorated so much (he is 94 years old) that it became necessary to dilate various **constrictions in his coronary arteries**. He has had heart problems since he was a child. By the end of 1994 there were periods of **extremely high blood pressure** which was supposed to be cured by medicines. All in vain!

The first dilatation of the constriction was successful and my uncle was able to lead a relatively pleasant life again. Sadly, only for barely three months. Then the attacks were worse than before. A particularly critical point (bend) had again become constricted and attempts to dilate this spot failed.

In spring 1996 my uncle was referred to Bad Oeynhausen where it was possible to open up this spot again minimally but only at the second attempt. My uncle was discharged.

As was to be expected, his health deteriorated month by month. More medicines were added and finally only constant spraying with "Nitro" kept him alive somehow.
Working in the garden or manual activities were out of the question. **Heart attacks and periods of high blood pressure characterised his daily life**. The thought of dying soon haunted him constantly.

This was the position until March last year when I received your book. After reading it feverishly one evening I ordered your basic vitamin programme. My uncle began taking it regularly in April. Only once, at the beginning did my uncle have a heart attack and was given potent drops by his doctor for such emergencies.

To date my uncle has had no need to take these drops! **His condition improved week by week**. He noticed that he could also do physical things again e.g. bending without falling over. Several weeks later my uncle got on his bicycle and made an (accompanied) **cycling trip without difficulty**. I could give you many more examples of the positive changes in my uncle.

Yours sincerely,

B.K.

Dear Dr. Rath,

Now that I have been taking your basic vitamin programme since September 1996, I would like to tell you about it today.

My dear wife sadly passed away – following heart attacks in 1970 and 1991- in February 1996. I have been suffering for a long time from **angina pectoris and have had several dilatations** (widening of the blood vessels), the last one about four months after the death of my wife. During my subsequent stay in hospital I read a small article in the "Welt am Sonntag" introducing your book. The next day I ordered the book from my bookshop and didn't rest until I had finished reading it. My GP, whom I asked for advice, advised me to take the preparation. I ordered it and waited.

Finally on the morning of my departure to the North of Germany the postman brought me the long - awaited package. I threw it into the waiting car and drove off. I began taking the basic course of treatment at the house of my friends in Husum. **After a week**, when I started my journey home, **I was already a new man**, I felt much better and drove all 900 km home without stopping. On the way there I had been forced to make an overnight stay.

From then my health improved again. I spent the following winter in Tenerife.

In the summer of last year I was again sent to hospital. The coronary angiograph only showed a slight deposit in one of the coronary arteries. **No further dilatation was necessary. In spring this year I had the laboratory results checked. The results were all excellent.**

I attribute the fact that I am so well again today, to your basic vitamin programme and for this I would like to give my heartfelt thanks to you, Dr. Rath, and your team. In the meantime I have told many of my acquaintances about the programme and I believe I can say, with success.

I am only sad that I didn't know about you and your product years ago; maybe I would have been able to help my wife.

Again, many thanks,

Yours sincerely

H.S.

Dear Dr. Rath,

I am 53 years old and eight years ago I had an **infarction of the anterior wall**. Since I constantly have feelings of anxiety and occasionally **high blood pressure**. On 1st March last year I began taking your basic vitamin programme.

After four to five months I felt **considerably more capable. I have stopped taking all medicines such as beta-blockers and ASS 100**.

Until now, no doctor has to date been able to explain why I had a heart attack. I did not have any of the risk factors, I am a non-smoker and I am not overweight.

Yours faithfully

V.S.

Dear Dr. Rath,

I am 47 years old and for two years have been suffering from **angina pectoris**. I was plagued by **sweating, shortage of breath, nausea, and pains in the thorax** and in my left arm.

Two months ago I began to take 3 *Vitacor Plus*, 2 *Arteriforte* and 2 *Enercor* each day. After only three weeks I only felt a slight pressure in the chest, **no more shortage of breath, nausea and outbreaks of sweat have totally disappeared.**

I should like to thank you, Dr Rath, and I will tell other people about your vitamin programme.

Yours sincerely,

Ursula Rösner

Dear Dr. Rath,

About two years ago I suffered **cardiac infarction** as a result of the passing away of my dear wife after a long period of care.

Since then I had constant problems with **angina pectoris, burning feeling with pressure and feeling of tightness in the chest**. By taking vitamins, minerals, trace elements and coenzyme Q10 which were recommended to me, I was able to keep the problems somewhat in check but could not stop them.

Of course I had completely changed my diet too but the angina pectoris symptoms, and above all the feelings of anxiety which prevented me from sleeping at night made the taking of medicines inevitable.

I am 78 years old and want to be rid of these complaints. As this was not possible through medicine and the fact that the attending **doctor advised balloon catheter treatment**, I decided to find a natural treatment to avoid surgery.

An acquaintance explained to me the effects of your cellular medicine vitamin programme. I also read your book and saw it as a last chance for me to avoid a coronary angioplasty operation.

At the beginning of May this year I ordered your vitamin programme and immediately began taking it daily with meals. After a week I increased the dosage as follows: early morning and afternoons one each of *Vitacor Plus* and *Arteriforte*. I continued to consult my doctor.

Already after only two weeks I noticed a distinct improvement. The burning sensation in my chest was reduced, the feelings of anxiety before going to sleep ceased and I no longer felt so weakened. **Since mid - June (after only a month) there have been no angina pectoris symptoms, I can live without fear again and my quality of life has been very much improved.**

I can now live completely without complaints and without taking any medicines, which I very gradually reduced and later stopped taking altogether. My doctor found a distinct improvement so that the **balloon catheter treatment now no longer seems necessary**.

You can imagine how pleased I am!

Yours, in gratitude,

Hansjoachim Schmidt

Dear Dr. Rath,

Ladies and Gentlemen,

During a catheter examination in February this year the cardiologist found that an **80 per cent constriction of the left coronary artery** (LAD) had **reduced to 50-60%** since May last year . This stenosis had not been dilated the previous year.

The doctors in attendance are aware of my participation in your vitamin programme. They agreed that they do not know of any other reason for the reduction in the stenoses.

Yours sincerely,

D.M.

Dear Dr. Rath,

Two years ago I suffered a **posterior wall cardiac infarction**. After my stay in hospital and subsequent curative treatment (cure), a two-vessel coronary disease was diagnosed at the subsequent cardiac catheter examination.

Following successful vascular dilatation by balloon catheter, new problems arose, in particular shortness of breath and faintness. Another opening of the vessels was refused, however. At the time I was very disappointed as I was now to live with a certain amount of risk.

Since February this year I have successfully been following your vitamin programme. **I feel very much better today and the problems have all but disappeared.**

I should like to offer you my thanks and shall also tell others with the same complaints about my experience.

Best regards,

R.L.

Dear Dr. Rath,

I am **35 years** old and I have been suffering acutely from constriction of the coronary vessels for six months. In November 1997 I suddenly had a **heart attack with fibrillation and respiratory arrest. I had to be resuscitated**, had balloon catheter treatment and a Stent*. It was a real shock to suddenly almost die at my age.

Since February this year I have been taking *Vitacor Plus* (2x2 daily) and *Arteriforte* (2x2 daily). **After four weeks the cholesterol level has fallen and my energy has increased**. Even sport is possible again to a normal degree (ten years ago I was still a professional football player!)

On 7th May this year I had another catheter examination: All blood vessels are open, blood results are good and I feel well.

I have told other patients of my experience and wish them the same progress as in my case.

Yours sincerely,

Dieter Kurth

*metal prothesis mesh which is implanted into the arterial wall to prevent the vessel from closing up.

Dear Dr. Rath,

I am 68 years old and for eleven years I have been suffering from **angina pectoris with piercing pains** in the left upper arm with any kind of movement, with feelings of panic and shortness of breath. Then I had a **heart attack**. The pressure pains, nausea, shortage of breath and the fear were unbearable.

Since April this year I have been taking the following Cellular Medicine formulas: *Vitacor Plus* one tablet three times a day and *Arteriforte* one tablet twice a day, also one tablet of *Enercor* twice for the last three weeks.

After three months there were no more pressure pains, no nausea and no panic attacks. What is particularly encouraging to me is that I can again take long walks, carry my shopping bag myself and tie my shoelaces without assistance. Inconceivable before!

Also I no longer need any Nitrospray and was able to cease taking other medicines. I am very grateful to you.

I probably don't need a bypass operation any more!

Yours sincerely,

Ingeburg Köhler

Dear Dr. Rath,

I heard and saw your video "The Chemnitz programme" in July 1997 and read your book "Why Animals Don't Get Heart Attacks" with interest.

I am 60 years of age. Since childhood I have had severe attacks of migraine (twice to three times per week) and from autonomic heart complaints since my youth. For about 20 years I have had **angina pectoris complaints, and high blood pressure with heart pains, rapid heart rate, pains extending to the shoulder and often to the hand**, swelling of the blood vessels on the left side of the neck, shortness of breath and panic attacks.

Since August I have been taking your Cellular Medicine formula, initially the basic formula *Vitacor Plus* three times a day and then from February this year also *Relacor*.

Since then my health has improved markedly, migraine only seldom and mildly. **No heart complaints any more!**

In 1974 and 1986 I had varicose vein operations in both legs. Even afterwards I still had circulatory problems, heavy legs, pain and felt agitated. These are now things of the past too!

I am very grateful to you and hope that you can help many other people.
All the best for you and your research!

Kind regards,

Crista Raderecht

Dear Dr. Rath,

In October I had my 84th birthday.

It was on 31st January 1991, it was very cold and I was out in the open. Suddenly severe pains shot through my chest and left arm. I went to the hospital in Gießen – **heart attack**.

In the ensuing period I was plagued by **heart pain**, particularly when there was a change in the weather. In December 1997 I began your basic vitamin treatment, 1 tablet each in the morning, at midday and in the evening. **After three months I had no more heart pain** and no more sensitivity to changes in the weather.

I can drive a car and cycle again, work in the garden and lift normal loads.

On 16th July this year I went for a check-up at the hospital. The ultra-sound showed that the **calcium deposits** in the region of the left ventricle had been **reduced**. The doctor examining me was amazed at the improvement in my condition.

I am well!

Yours sincerely,

Ernst Grün

Dear Dr. Rath,

Today as a user of your Cellular Medicine formula I would like to send you a report on my success.

I am 69 years old and have had **irregular rhythm of the heart (arrhythmia)** since 1983 and since then also a pacemaker. On 7th December 1996 I had a **heart attack**.

During the whole of last year I constantly had health problems and at least twice a month attacks of angina pectoris. My ability to cope was severely restricted. In November/December I suffered **extreme loss of energy** and constant heart pain. I could hardly raise my right arm due to the severe pain.

I was invited to see one of your lectures. Here I gained new hope and immediately ordered your products. Since mid December I have been taking three *Vitacor Plus* per day, since mid January this year also 3 *Diacor* and from mid February also 2 *Enercor*.

Already by Christmas last year I **no longer had severe pain**. In January I was almost without pain, my right arm had full movement again and **my general well-being had drastically improved**.

In contrast to the previous year, my health is good to very good. **I can do the gardening again almost without restriction**, which was inconceivable still in autumn 1997. In summary I can say that that the hope I gained from your lecture has been substantiated. I would like to express my thanks for this.

Yours sincerely,

P.H.

Dear Dr. Rath,

I am 72 years old and have suffered from **angina pectoris** for three years, characterised by severe pain behind the breast bone. After angioplasty (vascular dilatation by means of balloon catheter) a blood clot had formed. Consequently, **a by-pass operation** was performed. Two years later, **I again suffered from pain and shortage of breath, even with very slight exertion**.

Since 13th May this year I have been taking one of your basic formula *Vitacor Plus* tablets three times a day and **after only two weeks I was more energetic and had no shortness of breath. The recurrent heart pains with panic attacks have completely gone**, thanks to your Cellular Medicine.

I am already planning to give your book to my friends, relatives and neighbours and recommend your Cellular Medicine formulas. **I want to help in the battle against death from heart disease, and I know how valuable health is**.

Yours sincerely,

H.A.

Dear Dr. Rath,

I am **34 years old** and have been suffering from circulation problems for seven years.

Physical exertion would cause nausea and even vomiting. Other attendant symptoms were cold, stiff hands, faintness and circulatory collapse. Most of all I suffered from nausea and a feeling of lack of oxygen.

Since January this year I have been taking your Cellular Medicine formulas, namely *Vitacor Plus* and *Femicell*.

After two months the attacks of nausea and vomiting completely ceased. I have a **much better capacity** for particular physical exercise e.g. keep fit exercises.

My quality of life has improved considerably due to taking your vitamin treatment. I feel well and am happy to be able do something positive for my body. My thanks to Dr. Rath and his research team.

Yours sincerely,

Jim Mende

I am 64 years old and suffered a **heart attack** whilst in the best of health (slim, normal blood pressure and 159 mg cholesterol), so without warning. **After the heart attack** I often suffered **heart pain**, even when at rest, also **tiredness** and **oedema of the legs**.

Now, since I have been taking your basic programme (3x3 tablets) I have **no more heart pain**. **The oedemas in my legs have disappeared**. Above all the severe exhaustion I experienced during the day has disappeared.

But the most wonderful thing of all, is that I need no longer be in constant fear of a second heart attack (which is mostly even more dangerous). Here where I live, a man of 38 years of age died from the first heart attack and three men of between 40 and 50 died of the second, all near to where I am living.

I am eternally grateful to you for your research. I really hope you get the Nobel Prize.

With best regards,

E.W.

Dear Dr. Rath,

I am 58 years old and for several years have been suffering from occasional **heart pain.** The pains in the **left side of the chest periodically extending to the left shoulder and left arm** were agonising. Furthermore I often had problems with cold feet, influenza and angina.

I have been taking one tablet of your basic formula *Vitacor Plus* three times daily since August last year, and since February this year also *Arteriforte* twice daily.

After three months I noticed a considerable improvement in my state of health and capabilities. Furthermore, I can rejoice in having **no more heart pain and no more cold feet**. Since August last year I have had no more troublesome infections.

In brief, I feel good about myself again! I am very grateful to you!

Yours sincerely,

Wilhelm Raderecht

Dear Dr. Rath,

I am 62 years old and for about ten years I have suffered from **tightness of the chest and respiratory problems**. The following symptoms caused me a lot of trouble: tightness of the chest, shortness of breath, wheezing noises when breathing (not asthma, according to the doctor)

Six years ago I had a **heart attack** with no warning. Since the attack I suffer from **bouts of circulation problems, tight chest, difficulty breathing, high blood pressure (at times 210/100)**, periods of going hot and cold (head hot, body cold), panic attacks. I was found to have high cholesterol level.

I had to be sent to hospital by ambulance five more times (always in the evening and at night).

Since October I have been taking your Cellular Medicine formulas, namely basic formula and since this March, also *Metavicor* (3x1) and *Arteriforte* (3x2).

Soon I noticed an improvement in my health – actually, I have to say straight away, for I had no more attacks. After five weeks my blood pressure was normal (first reading up to 160, second always below 90). I could walk uphill, which hadn't been possible for years. Life is again worth living.

It was possible to halve the dosage of the medicines although it took a lot to persuade the doctor.

At one consultation, the latter said: If I didn't know better I would say you are quite healthy.

Dear Dr. Rath, you are the best thing that's happened to me in my life so far. I now want to live another 100 years to the full. Thank you.

Yours sincerely,

Doris Schlier

P.S. **I have now discontinued all my medicines** (ASS 100 and Xanef). My blood is thinned by Vitamin C, Vitamin E and beta-carotene and your treatment contains these constituents. My high blood pressure was reduced long ago due to your vitamin programme. I am well.

I am 59 years old and have been suffering from **heart and circulation problems** for three years. At the end of November 1995 I suffered **severe infarction of the anterior wall**. I had little chance of survival. There followed a rehabilitation period of seven weeks.

In March 1996 I began taking your basic vitamin treatment. Now after about 15 months **I notice an improvement in my general condition. I was able to reduce the amount of medicine I take, in consultation with my doctor. My blood pressure is stable.**

I learned about your vitamin programme from the information in your book. It should be recommended to everyone, young people in particular!
My family and many of my friends use your vitamin programme.

Yours sincerely,
Ulrich Plettendorf

Dear Dr. Rath,

I am 73 years old and for many years have had **circulatory problems**. Two years ago I had operations for **four bypasses**. Seven weeks later I had an operation to remove two thirds of my stomach.

I was so weak that I could no longer drive, not to speak of doing light jobs. My condition got worse and worse.

At the beginning of May this year I heard of your vitamin programme. I started slowly with *Vitacor Plus* and after four weeks also began taking *Arteriforte*. Now, after only six weeks, I feel much better, am driving again and can help my wife with the housework.

We are both so happy and my wife has now also begun your vitamin programme.

We thank you very much and hope that you can help many more people.

Yours sincerely,

K.H.M.

Dear Dr. Rath,

I am 63 years old and have suffered with heart problems for 12 years. I already had **two heart attacks and a bypass operation**. Three other arteries had already closed up again and were, I was told, inoperable as they were in a dangerous place.

In particular I suffered from **severe breathing difficulty, heart pain and feelings of oppression** due to which I repeatedly had to be taken to hospital by the emergency service. As a result of being in hospital and in my weakened condition I was almost helpless, and unable to do the housework.

Since April last year I have been taking your basic vitamin treatment, three tablets three times a day. **After only several weeks I was much better and in the meanwhile the heart pains and breathing difficulties with panic attacks have almost completely gone.**
I am so well that I can again do all my work in the house and even some work outside. I am so happy with this improvement!

Already six of my friends are taking the basic programme. I would like to thank you for your research.

Yours sincerely,

I.M.

Dear Dr. Rath,

Three years ago, at the age of 69, I suffered **infarction of the anterior wall**. After that, three dilatations were performed. At a further cardiac catheter examination I was to give my immediate consent to a bypass operation, which I did not do, however. And so I went home with mixed feelings.

I had resigned myself to the fact that I now had to go easier with everything. Walks were limited; **even at the slightest incline I had to stop and take a deep breath.** There was also a feeling of uncertainty, accompanied by mild faintness. Intensive physical activity exhausted me and brought me out in sweat. I also began to suffer from increased sensitivity to changes in the weather.

I have been taking *Vitacor Plus* and *Enercor* regularly now for eight weeks. **My general condition has considerably improved in this period**. I can take longer walks in the forest again along the same routes which exhausted me, or which I couldn't manage after the heart attack.
The feelings of uncertainty and faintness too have completely gone. I no longer need the strong cardiac stimulants.

Your research work is a blessing for me – and I hope for many others too. Thank you very much.

Yours sincerely,

Elli Meschkat

Dear Dr. Rath,

First of all I would like to explain my original situation: I am approx. 22 kg overweight. In December 1990 I had **a heart attack at the age of 44.** After an appropriate length of stay in hospital and subsequent rehabilitation treatment I was still classified by the doctors as severely "at risk from heart attack" and I was constantly given pharmaceutical preparations. This was mainly treatment in the form of **tablets to lower my blood pressure, level of blood fats, uric acid level (gout) and anticoagulants**. As a result of taking the medicines there was in fact no further heart attack, but the curative effect was next to nothing.

My physical condition was poor, I was susceptible to other illnesses, such as colds and often had pains in the chest.

Since January this year I have been taking the basic and tonic formulas of your vitamin programme regularly. **From March on things began to improve. My blood pressure, (initial reading 180/110 despite blood pressure tablets) dropped to the normal level of 140/90. I have completely stopped taking the pharmaceutical treatment for levels of blood fat, uric acid and anticoagulants**.

In 1996 I also developed diabetes. With a blood sugar level of 14 (250 mg/dl) I took one prescribed tablet per day, yet my sugar level remained just as high.

When I took the vitamins the sugar level fell to 7.0 (125 mg/dl). I intend, in consultation with my doctor, to stop taking the diabetes tablets as quickly as possible.

Since taking your vitamins my physical condition is much improved. I am considerably stronger. I notice this when climbing stairs, cycling, at work and when working in the garden and in the house.

As a "side effect" of taking vitamins, I have become resistant to colds.

I would like to thank you in this manner. I consider myself fortunate to have found out about your research in the field of cellular medicine. I am convinced that the new ways of eradicating the "diseases of affluence" will be recognised.

I assure you of my full support in the battle against restricted politics and the capitalistic interests of the pharmaceutical industry.

I wish you much success in your research.

Kind regards,

Christian Stoll

Dear Dr. Rath,

I am 52 years old and for eight years have suffered from **coronary heart disease with chest pain, tiredness, difficulty breathing and stress problems** – in a word; angina pectoris.

Since 1993 I have been taking your vitamin treatment, namely the basic formula (2 tablets three times daily). **After only four weeks my condition had improved.**

I had balloon catheter treatment in 1991. As a check, this year I had a cardiac catheter examination. Diagnosis: Excellent condition of the dilated vessel. **The coronary deposits have reduced since my taking of the course of vitamins.**

Yours sincerely,

K.K.

Appendix: Pictures of the cardiac catheter examination

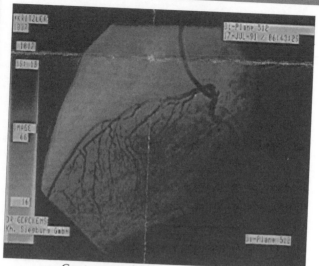

Contrast medium photo of the left
coronary artery dated 17th July 1991

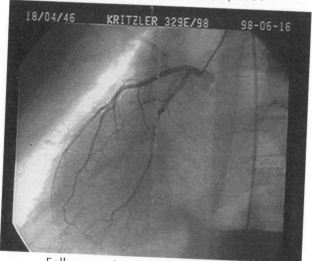

Follow-up picture of the left coronary
artery dated 16th July 1998

49

Dear Dr. Rath,

I am 65 years old. **For 17 years now I have been suffering from coronary vascular constriction and particularly pressure and tightness in the region of the heart and spasmodic pains. The medicine prescribed did not help.**

Since April last year I have been taking 1 tablet three times daily of your basic vitamin treatment.

My heart-rate stabilised and was markedly stronger after only one week. The above-mentioned complaints have almost completely gone.

I am very grateful for the help your Cellular Medicine gave me.

Yours sincerely,

Ilse Karig

Dear Dr. Rath,

I am 77 years old and in 1982 had **infarction of the posterior wall**. Also, my **left carotid artery was 50-60% closed, leading to dizziness and other problems**.

I have been taking your vitamin treatment for about one and a half years, regularly, 3-4 tablets a day. **Meanwhile, I am almost free of almost all the above mentioned complaints!**

As long as I live I do not wish to be without Dr. Rath's vitamin programme. My wife, (71 years old) is equally very pleased with the capsules she takes.

Yours sincerely,

H.J. and Mrs. H.

Dear Dr. Rath,

The state of my health has been characterised by a **heart attack** and severe **atherosclerosis** which have already meant four operations.

Now, after taking your vitamin treatment for quite a long time, I feel considerably healthier. **All test results for risk factors, including cholesterol, have considerably improved** and are in the" healthy" category.

Yours sincerely

Johannes Michel

Dear Dr. Rath,

I am 59 years old and **for 24 years have been suffering from abnormal heart rhythm, high blood pressure, breathing difficulties and pains in the chest**.

Since February this year I have been taking 1 tablet of *Vitacor Plus* three times daily and *Arteriforte* twice daily from the Cellular Medicine vitamin programme. After six months I noticed that **my heart-beat was normal and my blood pressure had normalised from 200/100 to 140/80. What is particularly welcome is the fact that I hardly ever have pains in the chest**.

Finally, I would like to point out that I was earmarked for a **bypass operation**. That has been **postponed indefinitely**.

Yours sincerely,

R.H.

Dear Dr. Rath,

This letter is intended to give an insight into our success with your Cellular Medicine.

Five years ago my husband, 90 years of age, was diagnosed as having **angina pectoris**. He had difficulty walking. After about 100 m he had **tightness of the chest and breathing difficulties**. The next step was always the **Nitrolingual Spray** which brought him temporary relief.

By chance we heard of your books, which gave us a lot of information. We acted promptly and ordered immediately several packets of your vitamin basic programme. **Three weeks later there was improvement. After a further two months my husband again is able to walk greater distances without having to fall back on the Nitrolingual spray. So, no more breathing difficulties and tight chest. Even his general condition has considerably improved**.

And now my own case: I am 80 years of age. Nine years ago I had a bowel operation (carcinoma of the colon) with subsequent chemotherapy. Since then I suffered from diarrhoea which was very unpleasant, and I could hardly undertake anything at all. All those medicines didn't help at all!

Then I thought, what helped my husband could also help me – which is what actually happened. After two months I noted an improvement and two months later I was rid of that terrible malady. Therefore the basic programme tablets also helped in my case.

We began on 15th May last year by each taking 2 tablets per day, and it has remained at that. It gives me pleasure to tell you all this, Dr. Rath.

Now we hope and trust that this vitamin programme will soon be available to the general public in Germany.

Yours respectfully,

Mr and Mrs K.

Dear Dr. Rath,

For 30 years I have suffered from **angina pectoris**. Now I am 60 years of age and on 20th December 1996 I had to undergo a cancer operation, followed by chemotherapy six times and tele-cobalt radiation 28 times. During and after this therapy I had more intense heart and circulation problems, low or severely fluctuating blood pressure.

Furthermore, I suffer from a congenital disease of the spinal column.

Then I heard about your Cellular Medicine from a friend and decided to provide my body with the vitamins recommended by you. On 2nd April this year I began by taking one tablet of *Vitacor Plus* per day, then also *Arteriforte* (one tablet once and later twice) from the second week on, since July 1998 also one *Femiforte*.

The result: **I was able to stop taking the medicine for circulatory disorders in July**. In addition, I had severe stomach pains from years of taking medicine for my spine. I was able to discontinue this medicine too. What was amazing was that my spine problems did not get worse as a result. That was never the case before!

And so I had the courage to go mountain climbing; I walked or climbed to five mountain huts near Oberstorf/Oberallgäu (altitude 1800 to 2000m above sea level) in July this year and was awarded the Oberstorf gold medal for climbing.

In contrast to the earlier period, when I always experienced pain in the region of the heart on inclines, I now had no problems.

I can only thank God for my good health for his loving guidance allowed me to hear about the results of your research. In the meantime, I have already been able to recommend your vitamin programme to many friends and acquaintances.

I thank you and wish you continued success and creativity.

Yours sincerely,

Regina Hübner

Dear Dr. Rath,

I am 47 years old. Three years ago I was diagnosed as having a **neglected anterior wall infarction (infarct of the anterior wall of the heart)**. The veins were blocked. I suffered from tiredness and weakness. In addition there were heart pains, which I tried to ignore.

I have been taking *Vitacor Plus* and *Enercor* from your vitamin programme regularly since the beginning of March this year. Six months later an ultrasound scan showed that a **blood clot**, of which I had not been informed, had **completely dissolved**.

Yours sincerely,

W.U.

Dear Dr. Rath,

I am 78 years old and suffer from the following: Since 1964, severe asthma, auditory collapse, cancer of the prostate, my veins are constricted and are supplied with blood up to only 30% in three places and up to 50% in five places. **Every 14 days I had severe heart attacks and had to go into hospital**. I had to take 24 medicines at intervals throughout the day.

I was made aware of your vitamin programme by my daughter. Since the end of January 1998 I have been taking 1 tablet of *Vitacor Plus* and 1 *Enercor* tablet twice a day. I wanted to stop after a week as I had pains in various places. I was advised to continue as it was probably a symptom of detoxification. I continued to take the formulas regularly.

It was good that I did! Today I can say that I am much better! No severe heart attacks any longer, no hospitalisation!

My doctor is also working with your Cellular Medicine. I pass it on wherever I am.

Thank you for your help.

Yours sincerely,

H. Adler

Dear Dr. Rath,

I am 66 years old and had a **heart attack** a year ago. **My capacity has been severely restricted ever since**.

Since May this year I have been taking one each of *Vitacor Plus* and *Relacor* three times a day. After only eight weeks my condition was already considerably improved. **I can again walk for several kilometres without complaint and climb moderate hills**.

When I was re-examined by my doctor, he found that the irregularities in my heart beat have also been reduced.

I can very much recommend your vitamin programme.

Yours sincerely,

Gerhard Hohmann

Dear Dr. Rath,

Thanks to my children I heard of the success of your research work and read the book "Why Animals Don't Get Heart Attacks – But People Do". For years I suffered from **angina pectoris and had to be repeatedly taken to hospital with severe heart attacks**. Panic attacks, breathing difficulties and pains characterised my state of health. Even short walks were difficult. Despite the doctors' efforts there was hardly any progress. I had to use Nitrolingual spray several times a day, which brought only brief relief.

Since September last year I have been following your recommendations and am taking *Vitacor*, *Enercor* and *Metavicor* daily. After only 5-6 weeks my condition was markedly improved. **I feel well all round and I am happy again**.

A few days ago I had a long-cherished wish fulfilled. I flew to Tenerife with my children and celebrated my 81st birthday there. **Without health problems; I am free of pain**. Thank you very much. I wish you strength and success in your work.

Ours sincerely,

E.R.

Dear Dr. Rath,

I am 58 years old and for a year I have suffered from **coronary disease** with severe stenosis (vascular constriction) which manifests itself as **painful throbbing in the chest** and simultaneous **breathing difficulties** even with slight exertion. Most of all I suffered as a result of the medicines which I had to take after a balloon catheter operation.

Since 19th May this year I have been taking your Cellular Medicine formulas. In the first month I took 1 tablet *Vitacor Plus* three times daily, then additionally 1 tablet *Arteriforte* twice daily. **The throbbing in the chest region subsided and I was again able to do my housework alone. After only three days this leaden tiredness disappeared**.

My doctor saw the good results from the vitamin programme and helped me to discontinue my medicines gradually. My skin problems also slowly subsided.

Yours sincerely,

G.A.

"Functional" heart complaints

Dr. Rath's Cellular Medicine Formulas for prevention and basic therapy

In many cases heart problems such as pressure on the chest and rapid heart rate occur without any constriction of the coronary arteries being detected in the examination.

In contrast to angina pectoris, the tight chest occurring predominantly during physical exercise, these heart complaints occur without any identifiable cause. They are therefore called "functional", which is tantamount to "cause unknown".

Medicine was not until now aware of any treatment for these heart complaints which were so unpleasant for the patients. Out of ignorance medicine christened these complaints "Heart neuroses" and the doctors prescribed psychiatric drugs, which often made the patients even more ill.

The following patients' reports document the fact that even the principal cause of "functional" heart complaints is lack of vitamins and other cell factors. Therefore even this common disorder has become causally treatable and will in future be largely unknown.

Dear Dr. Rath,

I am 49 years old and have been suffering since May last year from **functional heart problems**. It is triggered by sudden panic and develops into **high blood pressure, rapid heart rate and symptoms similar to a heart attack.**

Since May this year I have been taking one tablet three times daily of your basic formula *Vitacor Plus* and **noticed after only a month that the anxiety attacks had considerably reduced**. When they do still occur, my pulse and blood pressure remain constant. **I stopped taking beta-blockers and psychiatric drugs. My whole condition has improved**. I would not like to be without *Vitacor Plus* any more. A year of "anxiety" combined with many stays in hospital is now a thing of the past since June 1998.

I came across the vitamin programme as I worked myself to try to understand my illness and noticed from my own study that **disorders of a psychosomatic nature are often triggered off by stress**, but stress is a "robber of vitamins ". I thought, as a "heart patient", a prophylactic with your vitamin programme could do no harm.

The result is that I am now again free from symptoms.

Yours sincerely,

Dietmar T. Holtwiesche

Dear Dr. Rath,

I am 61 years old and since the birth of our three children (1960-1962) I have suffered **heart problems, stabbing pains in the chest and aching in my left arm. All the ECGs hitherto showed nothing, under exertion or relaxed.** On checking my pulse during senior citizen keep fit exercises I noted irregularities. Otherwise, in **stressful situations,** I suffer from the complaints described above, also from tiredness and loss of energy.

Since 20th April this year I have been taking your *Vitacor Plus* and *Metavicor,* one tablet three times daily. **After taking them for ten weeks, my physical and mental efficiency had markedly improved.** My lipoprotein(a) level improved from 40.5 mg/dl (on 27.3 this year) to 28.5 mg/dl (on 23.6).

Yours sincerely,

H.D.

Dear Dr. Rath,

I am now 45 years old and for about six years I have suffered from **circulation problems and indefinable heart pain.** This pain is accompanied by a great inner restlessness and aching in the left arm. Most of all I suffered from **the constant pains in the region of the heart. Troubled sleep** was associated with this and, hence logically, tiredness and bad temper during the day. Also, I noticed swelling of the legs and ankles in the evening. Despite all my efforts (relaxation training, extended walks etc.) there was no improvement.

From the 1st April this year I have taken your Cellular Medicine formula and in fact three *Vitacor Plus*, and two *Enercor* from May onwards. From June onwards I have also been taking two *Arteriforte*.

After three weeks, so in April, I was pleased to notice that **the pain in the heart region had considerably reduced** and I was able to sleep peacefully. In the following weeks the heart pain almost completely disappeared and I again had **the feeling of well-being I had lacked for so long.**

The swelling in the ankles was much less. Also other problems such as numb hands and cramp in the legs only occur very rarely. You can imagine how pleased I am about this.

Of course, I have told my GP about it and the referral to a heart specialist is now unnecessary.

I wish to thank Dr. Rath and his people from the bottom of my heart as it is simply wonderful to feel so healthy and well again.

I shall take pleasure in passing on reports of my good experience and this letter, whose publication I fully support, would be an opportunity for that.

Yours sincerely,

Birgid Frei

Notes

Stroke
Circulatory
disorders in the limbs

Dr. Rath's
Cellular Medicine formula
for prevention and basic therapy

Circulatory disorders of the brain, legs and other organs and parts of the body are caused by calcification of the arteries (atherosclerosis), in the same way as circulatory disorders in the region of the heart

The following patients' reports of success prove that circulatory disorders in general are almost as much a thing of the past as the effects of heart attack, stroke, leg amputation and others.

Dear Dr. Rath,

I am 79 years old and in August 1997 had the **first stroke** and in December 1997 the **second**. The resultant damage was **hemiplegia** in addition to **paralysis of the organs required for swallowing and speech** and therefore I needed a special diet.

Since March this year I have been taking your basic formula three times a day. After about ten weeks **the difficulties in swallowing subsided; I can eat again, say a few words, and I can walk again**.

I informed my doctor of this improvement and she was able to confirm it.I currently only have special diet as a snack. My mental health has improved and **after three months of *Diacor* my blood sugar has fallen from 12 (215 mg/dl) to 6 (108 mg/dl)**.

Yours sincerely,

Anna Wöhner

I am 36 years old and for six years have been suffering from constriction of the **carotid arteries (intracranial stenoses of the arteria cerebri ant. and the right media)** in addition to an excessive enlargement of the cranial artery (basilar cranial aneurysm). **The disease caused the following complaints: symptoms of paralysis in the left side of the body, no strength in the left side, fainting, speech difficulties.** Most of all I suffered from the fact that I couldn't learn and understand anything new and also from a feeling of helplessness.

I have been taking your Cellular Medicine formula, *Vitacor Plus, Arteriforte*, since the 29th May this year. I have noticed the following improvements after two months.

My left arm has **no paraesthesiae (abnormal sensations caused by circulation disorders in the brain), my memory is better, I am more energetic, I can again hold objects in my left hand and can open bottle tops.**

I informed my doctor of this improvement in my health and he was able to confirm that my general condition and blood count are good.

Yours sincerely

S.H.

Dear Dr. Rath,

A friend of my wife brought us your programme "Fight death from heart disease". After reading your brochures and hearing your audio-cassette I bought your book "Why Animals Don't Get Heart Attacks.." That was at the beginning of this year. In the meantime I am inspired by your Cellular Medicine research!

On 28th July 1996 whilst at work I had a cerebral infarction as the result of a **vascular occlusion in the brain.** "You were lucky, because the adjacent regions continue to supply blood via the fine capillaries of this area", said the senior hospital physician.

I myself did well after my stay in hospital. I showed no signs of paralysis. I only experienced fainting attacks which were twice very strong during the infusion period. Today I still have to take the medicines prescribed by the hospital! – Why, actually?

As improving the vascular system was paramount to myself and my wife, starting the basic programme with *Vitacor Plus* seemed reasonable.

2

After a month I also took *Enercor*. I later replaced this with *Arteriforte*.

My general condition has improved generally, difficulty breathing when climbing stairs or walking in the mountains have disappeared. I only rarely feel dizzy.

I have already told many acquaintances, friends and neighbours about your vitamin programme.

Thank you, Dr. Rath for your important research, which must benefit everyone and is affordable!

Yours sincerely,

Christoph Weigert

Dear Dr. Rath,

I am already having great success with your Cellular Medicine. I am impressed by your basic formula. In the case of my mother, who suffered **two strokes,** part of her speech was affected by the second. Since then she has been totally pumped full of medicines and infusions to thin her blood.

After some degree of persuasion, I was able to talk my mother round into also taking your basic vitamin treatment daily. She has now been taking the vitamin tablets (3x2) **for over a year with success and her speech is as good as new (apart from a few irregularities which remain).**

I not only attribute that to the medical treatment but also clearly to the vitamin supplement. For this reason I fully support your product.

I remain,

Yours sincerely

J.S.

Dear Dr. Rath,

I am 65 years old and for ten years I have suffered with **severe circulation problems. I had constant pain in my legs** and there was **no blood supply in my big toes**. Walking was sheer agony for me.

In October last year I began taking your Cellular Medicine formula, namely *Vitacor Plus* and *Arteriforte*.

After four months I could move my toes again! The pains were drastically reduced. I feel better month by month.

Indeed, I feel so well that in May this year I even painted my niece's house. Up the ladder, down the ladder!

Six months ago I could hardly walk without a stick.

Furthermore I had to take tablets for irregular cardiac rhythm and for high blood pressure for just as long. Three months ago I was able to discontinue both medicines.

I don't see a doctor these days.

Your vitamin programme has improved my quality of life so much that I would like to thank you from the bottom of my heart.

Yours sincerely,

Bruno Randszus

Dear Dr. Rath,

I am 53 years old and for 15 years I have had **problems with circulation in my legs**. This manifested itself in that I had severe pains in my calves particularly in the evenings.

Since 15th May this year I have been taking your Cellular Medicine formula, namely 1 *Vitacor Plus* three times daily and 1 *Arteriforte* twice daily. **After two weeks the pain in my legs was only slight and after three months the symptoms had disappeared without a trace!**

I am an adviser in your network and have had only good experiences! Thank God for Dr. Rath's vitamin programme!

Yours sincerely,

Josef Kohler

Dear Dr. Rath,

Today I want to say thank you. I have been taking your basic vitamin treatment and *Relacor* for about two months.

I have to say I was extremely sceptical. Somehow I expected overnight success in my condition. This was not immediately the case, until I suddenly noticed that the **circulatory problems in my legs had gone**.

I now again feel life in my legs. A completely new sensation, **to be able to stand and walk without difficulty**. All year I had been afraid of sunny days because then it was much worse.

So your Cellular Medicine formulas gave me a new start and I am now confident that everything else will go well.

Yours sincerely,

Maria Gröger

Dear Dr. Rath,

Today I can describe the first success of using your vitamin formula "*Arteriforte*".

I have to say, I am impressed by the results of your Cellular Medicine research and the resultant health treatment programmes. I had always hoped for such really effective products which tackle the problems at the root in a natural way. I immediately gave it my full attention.

I am 57 years old, tall and slim and have always tried to eat healthily. Despite my efforts in this regard, I developed **problems in the region of my left thigh**: **protruding veins**, "spider bursts", sensation of pressure accompanied by a nasty **itching, swellings over the ankle** and as a result, **socks cutting into the flesh, cold feet**. All this particularly in the evening when my cold feet always prevented me from sleeping.

After about three weeks of taking *Arteriforte* the itching and swelling have disappeared. The feeling of pressure has lessened considerably.

Finally I would like to express my gratitude and wish you every success in the broadcasting of the knowledge of your cellular medicine to which I am trying to contribute.

Yours sincerely,

Peter Chory

Dear Dr. Rath,

I am 42 years old and for five years have suffered from **circulation problems** which made me feel weak and tired. I constantly had **pain in my legs, shivering, lack of energy and tiredness**. On getting up in the morning already I had no energy.

I have been taking your basic formula *Vitacor Plus* three times a day for three months. **Six weeks later I noticed that the circulation in my legs was better and I had no pain. I am generally fit and more energetic than ever before**.

There are no traces of lack of energy or tiredness. I go through life with vigour.

I am happy that there are people like you who help mankind back to health using harmless vitamins.

Yours sincerely,

M.U.

Dear Dr. Rath,

I am 63 years old and for six years I have suffered from **circulation problems**, in particular **calcium deposits in the right carotid artery**. This condition often caused a **rushing noise in my right ear**.

Since autumn 1996 I have been taking your vitamin basic programme, as recommended in your book. After 18 months my circulation was tested and an EEG was performed by my neurologist.

The transformation was remarkable as the **arteries are completely free again and the noise in my ear has disappeared**.

I am overjoyed.

Yours sincerely,

R.M.

Dear Dr. Rath,

I am 50 years old and for two years have suffered from **circulatory problems**. I had **no sensation in my fingers.**

Since April I have been taking *Vitacor Plus* (3x1 daily) and *Arteriforte* (2x1 daily). **After nine weeks I could feel my fingers again**.

I am very satisfied with your vitamin programme. I feel very well.

Yours sincerely,

M.S.

Notes

3

Metabolic disorders and risk factors

- High cholesterol level

- High triglyceride level

- High lipoprotein(a) level

Dr Rath's Cellular Medicine formula for prevention and basic therapy

The facts about cholesterol and other secondary risk factors

Every second man and every second woman in Europe has an increased level of cholesterol, triglycerides, LDL (low-density lipoproteins), lipoprotein (a), and other risk factors in their blood. These blood factors are of lesser importance to heart and circulation, as the crucial risk factor is lack of vitamins and instability of the arterial wall. For this reason cholesterol and other blood factors are summarised as of secondary importance or secondary risk factors. Increased level in the blood of these risk factors is not, as previously believed, the cause of disease of heart and circulation, but rather the effect of disease.

Conventional orthodox medicine is restricted to reducing the symptoms of these secondary risk factors without treating the fundamental problem – the weak arterial wall. Medicines to reduce cholesterol currently prescribed for millions of people, do not treat the cause of heart and circulation disease. Moreover these medicines are dangerous: On 3rd January 1996 the American medical journal (JAMA) warned the public at large that all cholesterol reducing medicines to on the market at that time were carcinogenic.

Cellular medicine declared for the first time that cholesterol, triglyceride, lipoprotein (a) and other metabolic products are ideal molecules for the repair of the weakened arterial wall. When there is vitamin deficiency, the metabolic centre of the body, the liver, receives the signal to increase production of this repair-molecule. From there the repair molecules travel via the blood supply to the damaged areas in the arterial wall. Where there has been vitamin deficiency over many years, the repair of the vascular wall continues and leads to atherosclerotic plaque.

Where there is vitamin deficiency the liver receives the signal to increase production of repair factors to seal and stabilise the arterial wall

Principal cause:

Chronic deficiency of vitamins and other constituents
of Dr Rath's vitamin programme

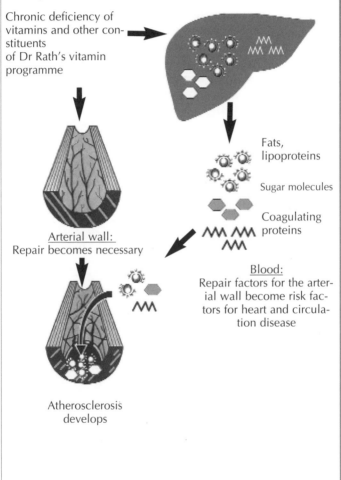

Fats, lipoproteins

Sugar molecules

Coagulating proteins

Arterial wall:
Repair becomes necessary

Blood:
Repair factors for the arterial wall become risk factors for heart and circulation disease

Atherosclerosis
develops

Dear Dr. Rath,

My first health check in 1995 (at barely 36 years of age) showed that my **blood cholesterol level was much too high** at 7.98 mmol/l (**310 mg/dl**). My doctor urged me to change my diet to **low fat food**, which I did.

Nevertheless I was only able to show a **slight improvement at my annual check-ups**. The level was just low enough for me not to have to take any medicine. From 1996 to January this year the level was 6.60, 6.63 and 6.88 mmol/l (around 260 mg/dl). I was not able to reach maximum 5.7 mmol/l (220 mg/dl) so I had to have a check-up every four months.

At the beginning of this year I began to take *Vitacor Plus* regularly, two to three tablets daily. Because of this the results of the cholesterol test on 11th May were **for the first time in the allowable range, i.e. 4.8 mmol/l (190 mg/dl)**.

In addition, I feel much less susceptible to infection and this year avoided the cold, occasional bronchitis I normally suffer in spring. I am convinced that this success is due to sufficient supply of vitamins and shall continue to take *Vitacor Plus* as a dietary supplement.

Yours sincerely,

M.L.

Dear Dr. Rath,

I am 43 years old and for three years have suffered from **high levels of cholesterol and triglyceride.**

I have been taking one tablet each of *Vitacor Plus* and *Metavicor* regularly three times a day since April this year.
The level of cholesterol fell from 264 mg/dl to 185 mg/dl and triglyceride from 246 mg/dl to 134 mg/dl in only three months.
I was not able to achieve this through diet. With your vitamin programme it was no problem.

I am impressed!

Yours sincerely,

Karin Anger

The mmol-l-value must be multiplied by 40 to convert the blood cholesterol level from millimol per litre (mmol/l) to milligrams per decilitre (mg/dl)

Dear Dr. Rath,

I am 68 years old. I have suffered from **coronary vascular disease** since 1985. On 22nd January 1988 I had to have a **triple aorto-coronary vein by-pass operation**. On 29th January 1989 another aorto-coronary bypass operation had to be performed due the unsuccessful by-pass implant on the coronary sinus.

When I read your book "Why Animals Don't Get Heart Attacks", my wife and I began your basic vitamin programme in March last year.

I have noticed the following changes in my condition:

Risk factor **lipoprotein (a)**
Result on 13./17.2 last year : 151 mg/dl
Result on 20./21.1 this year : 96 mg/dl.

HDL cholesterol ("good" cholesterol)
Result on 13.2 last year : 35 mg/dl
Result on 7.9 this year : 57 mg/dl.

Yours sincerely,

E.K.

Dear Dr. Rath

Before I began your vitamin programme my **cholesterol level was 320 mg/dl. Now it is 180 mg/dl**.

Furthermore, the **triglyceride level and HDL to LDL cholesterol balance is also normal. Above all my lipoprotein(a) level fell from 15 to 1 mg/dl.**

I will continue to take your vitamin treatment as long as I live.

Many thanks for your research into a natural way of reducing the risk for heart and circulation.

Yours sincerely,

M.R.

Dear Dr. Rath,

On 30th November 1973 I was involved in a serious traffic accident and suffered a multiple fracture of the left thigh, fracture of the condyle of my right shinbone and concussion.

That was the beginning of my suffering. Quite apart from several inconsistencies regarding "doctors' skills" in the treatment, my **left pelvic vein** simply **closed up** as a result of lying with my left leg in the air for ten weeks. The result was **post-thrombotic syndrome** in the left leg leaving me unable to work. 35% permanent damage to the body. Since then I received regular orthodox treatment from several doctors. Result: A causal treatment of this syndrome was never instigated from the start. The best advice from one surgeon brought relief to these complaints by prescribing support hosiery, due to "weak veins".

In 1990 I had to go to hospital due to pains in the hollow of the knee. The X-rays showed thrombosis. I was discharged after three weeks, and was then well and truly in the doctors' clutches! Medicines such as "Falitrom" almost turned me into a haemophiliac.

Bit by bit **new medicines were added for the metabolic problems**. In December last year it rapidly got worse. My doctor told me that the prescribed medicines were not helping. She said something about **"metabolic syndrome"** and "considerably limited", I would have to resign myself to the fact that it would not get better.

On 22nd December however a new life began. A life worth living! After being examined by a non-medical practitioner, for the first time I cut out Christmas goose, beer and many other favourite fattening foods from my diet. Nine of the 18 blood test results were abnormal, some were critical; high blood pressure, sugar, triglyceride levels were so high that the cholesterol level was not possible to determine etc, etc., etc. Eight of the nine abnormalities were in order again after a short period of natural therapy.

From May this year I then began your vitamin programme, namely *Vitacor Plus, Arteriforte, Metavicor* and *Diacor*. **After three months only the high blood sugar level remained. And this too had almost reverted after a further month**. Now in August the good results were confirmed at a check-up.

Over the last few months I have discontinued all medical treatments without any renewed worsening of the blood test results. Since December last year I have lost 21 kg in weight. At the same time the frequent bleeding of the eye, nose and gums has completely disappeared.

And **best of all, I again feel healthy and strong**. I am now working on eradicating forever the problem of heart and circulatory diseases for my family and myself. I look forward to the future with optimism! Thank you!

Yours sincerely,

Hans-Jürgen Baumann

Notes

4

High blood pressure

**Dr. Rath's Cellular Medicine
Formula for prevention
and basic therapy**

High blood pressure –
the medical breakthrough

10 million people in Germany and over 100 million people worldwide suffer from high blood pressure. This is the most widespread disorder of all heart and circulation problems.

Conventional orthodox medicine admits that in over 90 per cent of cases, the causes of this disease cannot be explained. A special diagnostic term was even invented for this "high blood pressure for reasons unknown", which disguises this fact: "Essential hypertension". As a result conventional medicine is restricted to using beta-blockers, diuretics and other medicines to treat the *symptoms* of high blood pressure but not the actual cause.

Modern Cellular Medicine constitutes a breakthrough in the research into the cause, prevention and supportive treatment of high blood pressure. The principal cause is a chronic deficiency of vitamins and other cell factors in millions of cells of the arterial walls. This leads to tension and thickening of the arterial walls, reduction in the diameter of the vessel and hence automatically to an *increase* in blood pressure.

Natural prevention and causal therapy of high blood pressure therefore consists in optimum dietary supplements in the form of vitamins (particularly Vitamin C) minerals (in particular, magnesium) and amino acids (in particular arginine). Reduced tension in the arterial wall leads to expansion of the internal diameter of the blood vessels and thus to *reduction* in blood pressure.

The following letters from blood pressure patients vividly confirm this medical breakthrough. Cellular Medicine is now bringing an end to this endemic disease.

Cellular Medicine and high blood pressure

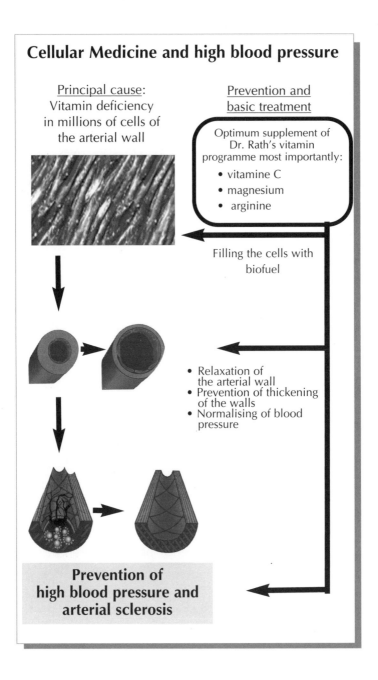

Principal cause:
Vitamin deficiency
in millions of cells of
the arterial wall

Prevention and
basic treatment

Optimum supplement of
Dr. Rath's vitamin
programme most importantly:

- vitamine C
- magnesium
- arginine

Filling the cells with
biofuel

- Relaxation of
  the arterial wall
- Prevention of thickening
  of the walls
- Normalising of blood
  pressure

**Prevention of
high blood pressure and
arterial sclerosis**

Dear Dr. Rath,

My aunt, (70) had **severe problems with high blood pressure** (systolic values 180 to 200). **She could not tolerate the chemical antihypertensives due to the side-effects**. She was quite desperate. I therefore recommended to her your basic vitamin programme which she has now been taking for about four months. For one month she has also been taking "*Relacor*", 1 tablet three times a day.

The vitamin formula was effective and the upper value for blood pressure is on average 140 or 135, so has reduced considerably.

Her doctor looked at my aunt's chart and was very surprised and **pleased with the results** from taking "*Relacor*". He immediately noted the address on the package.

Yours sincerely,

Arnold A. Neumann

Dear Dr. Rath,

I am **42 years** old and for two years have been suffering from **high blood** pressure. This condition, **at 150/100**, was treated with beta-blockers (atenolol 25). **Oedemas (water accumulation) in my calves really got me down.**

In June of this year I began taking one *Vitacor Plus* tablet three times a day and the same dosage of *Relacor*. After four weeks I tripled the quantity of *Relacor*. **After seven weeks my blood pressure normalised at 130/90 and the oedemas had noticeably reduced.**

Now neither beta-blockers nor other medicines are necessary.

Yours sincerely,

Harald Zastera

Dear Dr. Rath,

I am 48 years old and for three years have suffered from high blood pressure of 170 over 98. Most of all I suffered from **headaches** and **palpitations**. The doctor prescribed Xanef 5 mg twice daily.

For two months I have been taking one *Vitacor Plus* three times daily and the same dosage of *Relacor* additionally for one month. **My blood pressure is now 130 over 80. Wonderful!**
I no longer get headaches and my heart is now much more regular. There is no unpleasant palpitation. Also, I have noticed better circulation in my whole body and head. I can concentrate better, am better able to deal with stress. **In short, my general state of health has improved considerably.**

I shall continue to take your vitamin treatment as I have as yet found no doctor who can really help me.

Yours gratefully,

Anna Szczepaniak

Dear Dr. Rath,

I am 59 years old and for 18 years have suffered from **high blood pressure** with attacks of nervousness and dizziness. **Sexual inadequacy** has also troubled me greatly for three years. The medicines prescribed by the urologist did not help at all. In February this year I began taking your Cellular Medicine formula, *Vitacor Plus*, twice a day and *Relacor* one tablet three times a day. **My blood pressure changed after only nine weeks from 200/110 to 145/90. My love life is also a success again.**

Yours sincerely,

Manfred Szanzeitat

Dear Dr. Rath,

I am 61 years old and for 17 years have suffered from **high blood pressure. Dizziness** and **headaches** were the troublesome accompanying symptoms. My **blood pressure was 160/100**.

I have been taking your Cellular Medicine formula since January this year, namely *Vitacor Plus*, *Relacor*, and *Femiforte*, one tablet each three times daily.

Now after six months I feel considerably better and my blood pressure has dropped to 132/72. I now only take half a tablet for blood pressure and hope to discontinue this soon.

I am very grateful to you and will continue to recommend your vitamin programme.

Yours sincerely,

E.S.

Dear Dr. Rath,

I am 55 years old and **for 30 years have suffered from hypertension** (high blood pressure) and varicose veins. For years the high blood pressure was treated with medicines. In January this year I was admitted to hospital with **hypertension and thrombosis, blood pressure 230/130**. I also suffered a lot from swollen legs.

In May I began your basic formula *Vitacor Plus,* one tablet three times a day. Since June I have also been taking *Relacor,* one tablet three times a day, and *Arteriforte*, one tablet twice a day.

After about eight weeks my blood pressure stabilised to 130-140/85-90.

I was able to stop taking all but one of the medicines. I have no more problems with my legs and my varicose veins are not so severe as before.

I feel well again through taking your Cellular Medicine formula and can enjoy my professional life once more.

Yours sincerely,

R.S.

Dear Dr. Rath,

I have been taking **your vitamin treatment for nine weeks due to slight hypertension** (high blood pressure). I am 68 years old and **have already achieved normal blood pressure**. I am currently aspiring to the optimum 139/83 obtained in the HOT study.

In the last few days **I was able to halve the dosage of my ACE inhibitor (Lisinoporil) without my blood pressure increasing**. With the reduction of ACE inhibitors several **unpleasant side-effects** in the stomach and intestine also **disappeared**.

What prompted this experiment was the clinical study recorded at the end of the book "Why Animals Don't Get Heart Attacks" and the results mentioned there of the UCT (electron beam tomography) scan, which is sadly still not adequately available in Germany.

I have meanwhile been able to convince several friends of your vitamin programme and they are now too using it for their health.

I wish you every success in your work.

Yours sincerely,

Dieter Rehberg

Dear Dr. Rath,

I am 66 years old and for 15 years have suffered from "**essential high blood pressure**" with the following symptoms: shortness of breath, pressure in the region of the heart, feelings of stress and uneasiness. My cholesterol level is also high.

I have been taking your vitamin basic programme (3x1), *Relacor* (3 x1) and *Metavicor* (2 x 0,5) since March this year.

After only six weeks my blood pressure was less high, there was no sign of the high-pressure period at midday and in the evenings, in contrast to before, it only rose slightly.

Over time **my blood pressure returned to normal – despite halving the beta-blocker medicine**. Perhaps soon I won't need any beta-blockers at all any more.

I feel more active, younger. The formulas noticeably heal the circulation system bit by bit.

Yours sincerely,

I.L.

Dear Dr. Rath,

I am 78 years of age and have suffered from **high blood pressure** for 20 years. Also **cardiac insufficiency with water retention in the legs** and dizziness caused me a great deal of trouble.

For four months I have been taking your Cellular Medicine formula, *Vitacor Plus*, *Enercor* and *Relacor*, each three times a day.

After only four weeks my blood pressure fell – you can see this positive development yourself on the enclosed diagram.

The **water accumulation** in my legs has also **reduced** and I enjoy walks more again and **sleep better at night**.

My doctor has confirmed the improvements and consequently **discontinued the blood pressure tablets**.

My thanks to you and your team!

Yours sincerely,

I.L.

After 20 years of high blood pressure

Natural reduction in blood pressure
from 205/98 to 155/85 with
Vitacor Plus, Enercor and Relacor.

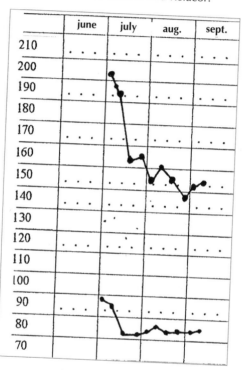

Dear Dr. Rath,

My blood pressure has been rather low all my life, then for the last few years I have suffered from **high blood pressure**: My legs, arms and hands go numb.

The doctor treating me prescribed the beta-blocker Metoprolol retard –Ratiopharm (one 200mg tablet per day).

From the beginning of May this year I have also been taking your dietary supplement *Relacor* and *Vitacor Plus*, 3 x 1 each.

Within 14 days the first reading of **my blood pressure dropped from 180 to 140**; it is currently 130! All the measurements were taken by my doctor.

Furthermore I can say that in addition, **my well-being and efficiency have been able to be increased**.

I would like to thank you very much.

Yours sincerely,

E.H.

Dear Dr. Rath,

I have been a plasma donor for two years. Each time I donated, my blood pressure was taken. The results were recorded on a weekly basis (same day, same time).

I have become **concerned about my blood pressure results** as they were at the upper limit allowed for donating blood e.g.

02.09.97	155 over 95
16.10.97	190 over 100
26.12.97	**165 over 90**

At the beginning of this year I learned of your vitamin programme from an acquaintance and have been taking two *Vitacor Plus* tablets twice daily. My blood pressure has, to my delight, improved greatly since then e.g.

10.04.98	130 over 85
02.07.98	140 over 80
12.08.98	**130 over 80**

I shall continue taking *Vitacor Plus*.

I am happy to **support your work which is so important for the health of mankind.** It feels good, too, to be able to help oneself and others.

I wish you every success in attaining your high objectives.

Yours sincerely,

R.E.

Dear Dr. Rath,

I am 67 years old and for seven years I have had problems with my circulation following inflammation of the cardiac muscle. I had **unstable blood pressure** constantly which fluctuated between normal and **high blood pressure**. My blood pressure has almost always been high ever since January.

In June this year I began taking *Vitacor Plus*, *Enercor* and *Relacor* from your Cellular Medicine programme. After only a month I noticed a relative **stabilisation of my blood pressure**. There was also an essential improvement in my well-being and headaches were only infrequent.

I was able to stop taking "Isoket" and my blood pressure medicines meanwhile.

Since the beginning of August this year I have also been taking *Arteriforte* for a few varicose veins needing treatment. I am confident here also.

Yours sincerely,

G.K.

Dear Dr. Rath,

I am 41 years old and for six years have suffered from **high blood pressure**. I had problems getting to sleep, insomnia and weariness during the day. More than anything I suffered from severe palpitations when lying down and a pulse of 80 whilst at rest.

Since February this year I have been taking *Vitacor Plus* and *Relacor*, each three times a day. Before this, I had gradually stopped taking the prescribed beta-blockers*. After one day of severe withdrawal symptoms, everything normalised, even my pulse. After four weeks I had **no problems with stress** any longer.

I feel well and am happy to have found a solution to supply my body with the vitamins it lacks in addition to healthy food and to be able to live without chemicals.

Yours sincerely,

E.B.

* Note: Please only reduce your heart medicines in consultation with your doctor.

Dear Dr. Rath,

I am 47 years old and have suffered from **high blood pressure** for ten years with the following symptoms: dizziness, tightness of the chest and tiredness, also however disturbance of the cardiac rhythm and increased heart rate.

Since November last year I have been taking *Vitacor Plus* and *Relacor* (three times a day). After four months the tightness in the chest disappeared, the dizziness had gone, my efficiency has increased and I can again get out of bed quickly in the morning.

The first reading of my blood pressure has fallen from 180 to 135.

I have told my doctor about your Cellular Medicine programme, but got no reaction. His scepticism only subsided on seeing the good results.

By taking Cellular vitamins **I have discontinued my blood pressure medicine**, and could present my doctor with the full proof.

The pharmaceutical tablets and their side-effects did not help me. I wish your team continued success, and many thanks.

Yours sincerely,

A.H.

Dear Dr. Rath,

I am 52 years old and for 10 years have suffered from **high blood pressure** and **bleeding gums**. My blood pressure was 140/92 and my gums bled constantly when cleaning my teeth or eating an apple.

In April this year I began your basic programme *Vitacor Plus* and since then I have been taking 1 tablet three times a day.

After eight weeks I had **no bleeding of the gums** any more, not even after vigorous brushing. Also, a medical check-up showed that my **blood pressure is now 120/80**.

Yours sincerely,

Hilmar Kickel

* Note: Hundreds of years ago, the first indication of vitamin deficiency in seafarers was bleeding of the gums.

Dear Dr. Rath,

I am a **high blood pressure patient**. Values of 160 over 100 were the order of the day and I was treated with medicines. As I showed a certain degree of loss of drive, I simply stopped taking the blood pressure medicine. A check-up at the doctor's again showed excessive blood pressure, and I had to take medicines again.

It was a vicious circle, until one day, by chance, I saw the video of the "Chemnitz programme". Subsequently I read your book Why Animals Don't Get Heart Attacks ("Warum kennen Tiere keinen Herzinfarkt") and so came across your Cellular Medicine formula. I took 2 vitamin tablets three times daily.

After two months my blood pressure stabilised. Since *Relacor* is now also available, I take one *Vitacor Plus* and one *Relacor* three times a day.

I stopped taking my blood pressure medicines bit by bit, and then completely. My blood pressure is now **completely normal at 140-146/86-88**.

I am impressed and at the same time convinced of the effectiveness of your vitamin programme.

After having such success myself, I passed your book on to a colleague. He also has problems with blood pressure and in addition the doctor has diagnosed **inflammation of the mucous gland**. He complained of **severe pains in the knee and had to be treated as an in-patient**. Since mid December he has been taking the basic formula three times a day and has been **free of pain and complaints since the end of February**.

With this account I should like to express our gratitude to you combined with the hope that you will provide us with yet more background information.

In this way we will be able to support your work towards the building of a new health system to win the battle with death from heart disease.

Yours sincerely,

W.B.

Dear Dr. Rath,

Our mother has **suffered from high blood pressure for over 20 years**. Although she had antihypertensives as she had already had two mild strokes, it was not possible to get her blood pressure under control.

Since May, on my advice, she has taken Coenzyme Q10, from July onwards your vitamin programme and Depressan.

Now she only takes your vitamin programme and no Depressan.

Everything has turned out well!

Thank you!

Christina Schönfelder

Dear Dr. Rath,

I have suffered from **high blood pressure** for five years and have to take medicines every day. I have been taking *Vitacor Plus* and *Relacor* for five weeks.

At the outset of the treatment, my blood pressure was **180/115**; after taking it for 14 days, it had fallen to 165/95 and the **last result was 130/80**. I attribute this improvement to taking the vitamins, will continue to take them and will endeavour to inform even more people about the vitamin programme.

Yours sincerely,

B.D.

Dear Dr. Rath,

I am 73 years old and **for seven years have suffered from high blood pressure**. This has already been the cause of a heart attack. Furthermore I suffered a lot from tiredness, heart pain and dizziness.

Since 15th April this year I have been taking *Vitacor Plus* and *Relacor* from your Cellular Medicine programme.

After 19 weeks I noticed that I **no longer had heart pain** when walking uphill, for example.

My blood pressure too had normalised and stabilised and my doctor advocates continued treatment with the formula.

Yours sincerely,

A.O.

Dear Dr. Rath,

At the age of 37 I am suffering from **high blood pressure** and from cancer of the abdomen.

Cancer announced itself by extreme pains in the back and lower abdomen. I was plagued by the constant fear that this disease would spread.

I have now been taking your Cellular Medicine formula, *Vitacor Plus*, 1 tablet three times daily and *Femicell*, 1 tablet twice daily for the last three months.

After only two weeks my blood pressure normalised. I feel supremely well. My fear has subsided as it feels good to know that my body is getting everything it needs.

I learned of your vitamin programme from a friend. I will take it all my life so that the cancer doesn't get another chance!

I have already and will in the future recommend it everywhere; the effect was fantastic.

Yours sincerely,

Sonja Baggenstos

Dear Dr. Rath,

I am 51 years old and am writing this letter in gratitude for the help given to me by your Cellular Medicine.

Ever since I was 28 I have had constant medical treatment for **high blood pressure**, angina pectoris and high cholesterol levels. Despite various medicines **my blood pressure was seldom below 150 /100**. There was no organic cause of my constant heart pain and increasing loss of performance.

Despite taking ever more different medicines to improve circulation and reduce blood pressure, through beta-blockers and medicines to lower the cholesterol level my condition continued to worsen. I had constantly swollen legs. I suffered increasingly from **tightness of the chest and difficulty breathing**. Worst of all was at night when I was awakened by **rapid heart rate**. During the day I was in constant fear of the next heart attack.

Due to the inadequate curative effect of the medicines, treatment of my complaints became increasingly expensive. For years I have been searching for other solutions or treatments which are more digestible or free from side effects. Increasingly I noticed the undesirable and harmful side-effects of the drugs. Your books ""Nie wieder Herzinfarkt" (No more heart attacks) and Why Animals Don't Get Heart Attacks ("Warum kennen Tiere keinen Herzinfarkt") clarified what I up to that point had only suspected or had not sufficiently understood about the connection between vitamins and health and the treatment of my illnesses.

I immediately stopped taking the medicines to lower my cholesterol level.

In December last year I began your basic formula *Vitacor Plus* which I supplemented after four weeks with *Arteriforte*. I also took *Enercor* and *Relacor*, each in the stated dosage, from the third month.

The effect was amazing. After only two weeks of taking *Vitacor Plus* I felt noticeably better. After many years I cold sleep through the night again. Two weeks later I was completely free of pain.

Since then my efficiency has also significantly improved. I do not tire so easily and can cope with stress again. **I can again go on strenuous walks and climb stairs without difficulty**. This was not the case before, despite taking medicines and various dietary supplements.

I am certain it was only your vitamin programme and the unique combination of your formula which made my rapid improvement possible. I am writing to you now, though I have been completely free of pain for several months. **I had to take medicines for more than 22 years. And so I was afraid that the improvement without medicines might only be temporary.** I am convinced of the effectiveness of your vitamin programme. Meanwhile I have been able to **discontinue taking all the medicines. My blood pressure is already 130/80 mm Hg. My cholesterol level is normal.** I feel very good generally.

I am happy that your vitamin programme exists. Thank you for this.

Yours sincerely,

Udo Werner

Notes

5

<u>Cardiac insufficiency</u>

- **Oedema**
- **Shortness of breath**
- **Loss of performance**

**Dr. Rath's
Cellular Medicine formula
for prevention
and basic therapy**

Cardiac insufficiency – the medical breakthrough

Millions of people in Germany and Europe suffer from a weak heart (cardiac insufficiency) with breathing difficulties, oedemas and severe loss of performance. The only way the epidemic spread of even cardiac insufficiency can be explained is that up until now there has been no or insufficient knowledge of the principal cause of this disease.

Conventional orthodox medicine is essentially restricted to treating the *symptoms* of cardiac insufficiency. Medicines (diuretics) are prescribed to drain and flush out the water that accumulates in the body of patients with cardiac insufficiency due to reduced pumping efficiency of the heart. As the actual causes of cardiac insufficiency are not remedied, the prognosis is extremely poor. If a patient is diagnosed with cardiac insufficiency today, his chances of still being alive in five years are only 50%! For many cardiac insufficiency patients a heart transplant is their last hope, but most patients die without ever having such an operation.

Modern Cellular medicine offers a major breakthrough in the research into the causes, prevention and causal treatment of cardiac insufficiency. The most common cause of cardiac insufficiency is lack of vitamins and other cell energy factors in millions of cardiac muscle cells. This lack of bioenergy in the cardiac muscle reduces the pumping efficiency of the heart and leads to shortness of breath, oedema and rapid physical exhaustion.

The following letters from patients with cardiac insufficiency vividly confirm this medical breakthrough. Cellular Medicine is now helping to eradicate this endemic disease.

Cellular Medicine and Cardiac Insufficiency

<u>Principal cause:</u>
Vitamin deficiency
in millions of cells
of the cardiac muscle

<u>Prevention and
basic treatment</u>

Optimum supplement of
Dr. Rath's vitamin
programme, Principally:

- Vitamin C
- Coenzyme Q10
- Carnitine

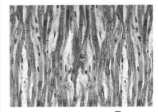

Filling the cells
with biofuel

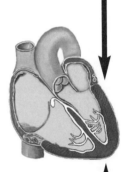

- Improved elasticity of
  the cardiac muscle cells
- Increased pumping effi-
  ciency of the cardiac
  muscles
- Reduction of oedemas
  and shortness of breath
- Improved physical per-
  formance

**Prevention and
basic therapy for
cardiac insufficiency**

Dear Dr. Rath,

This letter should be considered a note of thanks. I can tell you that your vitamin programme offers a good chance of survival.

As for me, I am 47 years old and have been **100% unable to work since my heart attack on 29th March 1993**, since which time **I have hardly been able to undertake any physical activity**.

After the attack I was in the rehabilitation clinic and treatment with tablets began. That went well until 1995, then I took up smoking again. My body weight was mostly around 100 kg, my height 1.71 m. So, constantly 30 kg overweight. Further problems arose from January 1996 which I dismissed as side-effects of the medicines and did not give too much thought to. Since this time, however, my efficiency and quality of life had been severely restricted.

I tried to activate my body's own power to heal itself. I stopped taking my medicines without medical support. Things went relatively well until the end of the year, but then I suffered absolute loss of strength. I had difficulty breathing and after two days of personal effort I was admitted to the Marienhospital in Bonn on 22nd January with symptoms of decompensation of the left side of the heart. I was fitted with a pacemaker. My heart was considerably enlarged.

After this it was revealed to me that I must be prepared to have a heart transplant.

For final clarification I was transferred to the University Hospital in Bonn. The diagnosis was severe restriction of overall pumping efficiency, incipient arterial hypotension, coronary heart disease with 50% extensive stenosis (constriction) and thrombosis (blood clot) in the region of the right and left atrium. On 13th February this year I was discharged, treatment with Marcumar being commenced prior to this however.

On 18th February I started taking steps towards rehabilitation. Since this point I have been taking a triple dose of the vitamin programme developed by yourself.

The check-up on 5th March showed a moderate reduction in heart size, **overall a significant improvement**. On 24th March, in contrast to the previous result, the pathological heart size had again been reduced and so too the diameter of the central pulmonary arteries. On 7th April again a significant reduction in heart size was recorded.

On 29th April I was admitted to the University Hospital in Bonn, as planned. No thrombosis could be found any longer in the right and left atrium. I was finally discharged. **The transplant is no longer necessary!**

Since starting your vitamin programme my physical performance has increased enormously and my quality of life is good again. I am convinced that your vitamin programme has helped. I want to say a big "thank you".

Yours sincerely,

Lothar Meiszner

Dear Dr. Rath,

My mother has become increasingly weaker since mid January this year. She could no longer get out of bed unaided, let alone get back in again. I had to feed her and sleep at her house to help her.

The GP diagnosed **cardiac insufficiency,** the pumping efficiency got weaker and weaker.

As the **water accumulation in her feet** was getting worse, the GP changed the water tablets from "Disalunil" to "Furantil". My mother also had to take "Pholedrin longo" and "Myofedrin". My mother rapidly lost weight, five to seven kilos in a week, as a result of the **change in medicines**. Her feet were no longer swollen but instead she was totally **weakened.** I, on my own account, stopped the tablets every four days. **The shortness of breath did not improve**, her blood pressure rose slightly to 100/70, the weakness remained.

Since the beginning of May I have been giving my mother, now 93 years old, one tablet of *Vitacor Plus* three times a day and also one *Enercor* twice a day.

Today we are amazed at my mother's recovery!

The shortness of breath is much better, the dizziness is gone, likewise the water accumulation in her feet.

Her strength is slowly returning, she gets up her-self and opens the door to receive visitors. **Her appetite has returned, she no longer needs to be fed. Blood pressure 120/80.**
Thanks to the Cellular Medicine formula!

My mother's state of health has considerably improved.

My mother and I would like to thank you, Dr. Rath, very much. Your research was not in vain. We are grateful that it is available to everyone.

Yours sincerely,

Else Weigert

Dear Dr. Rath,

My mother is 83 years old and for two years has suffered from cardiac insufficiency. She has already had two heart attacks. She suffers from **shortness of breath, accumulation of water in the lungs** and in the left leg and tiredness. Shortness of breath was the worst thing for her.

Since February this year she has been taking your Cellular Medicine, *Vitacor Plus, Enercor, Femiforte, Femicell* and *Arteriforte*. **After only a week she noticed that the shortness of breath had considerably improved**. The diagnosed severe lack of white and red blood corpuscles and low haemoglobin level (also indications of anaemia) had disappeared in two weeks of taking *Femicell*. The planned spinal cord scan therefore did not take place.

Her heart has recovered well and her blood count is again normal. **It was possible to reduce her heart tablets and she was able to stop taking the water tablets completely.**

All in all we can say that my mother is doing well for her age, thanks to Dr. Rath's vitamin programme.

Yours sincerely,

Anneliese Wallner

Dear Dr. Rath,

I am 53 years old and for two years have suffered from **cardiac insufficiency**. The effects were **shortness of breath, tiredness** and poor quality of sleep. Most of all I suffered from constant tiredness and the need to pass water in the night.

For three months now I have been taking one tablet of *Vitacor Plus* three times a day, and one *Enercor*, twice a day.

After eight weeks I noticed for example that **climbing stairs was not so much trouble** and the quality of sleep had markedly improved. What was particularly welcome was that the **need to pass water in the night had reduced** and my efficiency during the day had improved.

An ECG confirmed the improvement in the action of my heart.

It was possible to reduce the dose of "Strophantin".

Yours sincerely,

M.M.

Dear Dr. Rath,

I am 71 years of age and **have suffered for ten years from cardiac insufficiency**. The complaints I suffered from were **difficulty breathing when climbing stairs, periods of exhaustion and constant tiredness**. The most aggravating was the difficulty breathing with any exertion.

Since 12th July this year I have been taking your Cellular Medicine formula, one *Vitacor Plus*, three times a day and one *Enercor* twice daily.

After six and a half weeks I was more efficient and even climbing stairs wasn't so much of a problem any more. My general condition has much improved.

Yours sincerely,

M.St.

Dear Dr. Rath,

I am a practitioner in alternative medicine and would like to tell you about a patient who has been using your Cellular Medicine basic programme since July this year.

The patient was diagnosed with arterial **hypertension (high blood pressure)** in 1980, suffered an **anterior wall infarction** in 1996. Complaints since this time were **general debility, extreme tiredness, difficulty breathing and faintness when climbing stairs**.

In March this year a deteriorated **insufficiency of the left side of the heart (cardiac insufficiency)** with critical hypertension and thrombosis (blood clot) in the left atrium, plus sclerosis of the aortic valve (calcareous deposits in the cardiac valve) was diagnosed. Since then, dizziness and unsteadiness when walking have presented themselves, continued tiredness and faintness. The patient takes the anticoagulant Marcumar.

At the end of July he began taking *Vitacor Plus*, (3x1)

After only ten days he suffered no longer from attacks of dizziness. After 25 days he reported: climbing stairs is less strenuous, his customary after-lunch sleep has been reduced from 3,5 hours to 1 hour's rest.

The patient appears generally more alert. There have been **no more great fluctuations in blood pressure**.

The patient is now beginning *Arteriforte* (3x1)

Yours sincerely,

I.S.

Dear Dr. Rath,

My husband has been suffering from cardiac insufficiency for several years. He was often in hospital due to severe heart attacks and was treated with tablets repeatedly. Without success. My husband's stomach had a sensitivity reaction to the medicines so he ate less and less and lost weight.

About six weeks ago he was diagnosed with only 15% pumping efficiency of the cardiac muscle.

After my husband began your vitamin programme he improved from day to day. After only 14 days he could climb stairs again without having to stop on every second step. Even extended walks, which he had been unable to undertake for ages, are possible again.

We are so thankful to you, Dr. Rath, for this wonderful thing and tell all our relatives and friends about our experience with your vitamin programme.

Yours sincerely,

Cornelia Koth

Dear Dr. Rath,

I have been to hospital twice already with **severe cardiac insufficiency,** the last time being this spring, I was discharged with several medicines, among them Marcumar.

A short time ago I learned of your Cellular Medicine from a newspaper article and extensive information from you. I immediately ordered *Vitacor Plus* and *Enercor.*

First of all I took *Vitacor Plus* for a few weeks and felt the positive effect really quickly. *Vitacor Plus* gave me **the vital push for more strength and pleasure in dealing with even extraordinary challenges and tasks.**

By supplementing with *Enercor* I have now been able to **reduce my heart medicine to a minimum and stop taking Marcumar completely.**

I am so pleased and thankful for this and my husband and I will do all we can to support the use of vitamins.

Yours sincerely, and with best wishes for your courageous effort!

Maria Mühlmann

Dear Dr. Rath,

Eleven years ago I suffered a heart attack and had two bypasses. Despite the antihypertensives my blood pressure systolic reading was all too often above 200 and was seldom below 180. Later shortness of breath was detected and the heart specialist prescribed ACE-inhibitors. Later still **cardiac insufficiency was diagnosed.**

I had never heard the words cardiac insufficiency before. **The build up of blood in front of the left ventricle went as far back as the liver. For the next three years I only had a 50% chance of survival.**

The pumping efficiency was already so bad that a year ago I could only manage the second step with panting, the four steps only with two pauses.

On the other hand, I had to take Molsidomin three times a day. If I had forgotten one tablet, one or two hours later I was vividly reminded of it by tightness in the chest and difficulty breathing.

Two months after beginning your Cellular Medicine formula *(Vitacor Plus, Enercor)* I was no longer aware of such reactions and stopped taking Molsidomin completely.

That means only the vitamins could have the effect that the bioenergy was allowed to build up to improve the pumping efficiency which the restricting of the pharmaceutical pills had made possible.

I found this very interesting, for since my heart attack, I have swallowed some 25,000 tablets. You cannot get healthy like that.

My thin waxy skin which immediately used to start to bleed, is back to normal again. **The agonising daytime tiredness is gone. Also, I can now again climb the four steps like a healthy 66-year-old.** I went **uphill and downhill without complaint for two hours** on a school trip with my 9-year old daughter.

Also the medical examination showed that **the pumping efficiency is better and the heart has decreased five centimetres in size. My blood pressure is now 125/75 to 140/85.**

I thank you, Dr. Rath, from the bottom of my heart. I expect to prolong my life now with your knowledge.

With best wishes to you and your team,

H.N.

Dear Dr. Rath,

I am 78 years old and for three years have suffered from **Cardiac insufficiency** and circulatory problems. I was so weak that I could hardly walk.

I have been taking *Vitacor Plus, Arteriforte* and *Enercor* for a quarter of a year.

I can say that I now feel much better. I can again do small jobs in the house. I can already walk short distances accompanied, which was not possible before.

I am very happy and grateful for this and hope I will continue to feel better.

Yours sincerely,

L.M.

Dear Dr. Rath,

I am severely restricted due to my weak heart.
Furthermore, I had to be operated on both hands
for trapped nerves. Due to the fact that my GP
recognised this too late, not only did my hands
remain without sensation but also cold. Since taking your vitamin programme my hands are at least
warm again.

**I have been taking your treatment since then
and I am better.**

Before, I had to lie down again after 3-4 hours
spent upright (so, sitting or walking) due to my
weak heart; this is now only necessary after seven
hours.

I can now also take longer walks. Previously a
walk of 150 m, now 180 m. And all that without
the fear that it might harm me. I also feel stronger.

I am 99 years old. This is confirmation of Dr.
Rath's treatment at any age!

Yours, in gratitude,

R.B.

Dear Dr. Rath,

I am 62 years old and for five years have suffered from arteriosclerosis with arrhythmia and angina pectoris, pains in the chest and shortness of breath.

After a severe heart attack my ability to take stress was very severely limited and I suffered from constant tiredness and lack of energy.

Since mid-march I have been taking your Cellular Medicine formula, *Vitacor Plus,* and *Enercor.*

After only four weeks I noticed that my heart was beating more strongly, that there was also no disturbance in cardiac rhythm nor angina pectoris pain. I was able to climb the **stairs** to my second floor flat quickly again and manage it **without difficulty breathing,** even with heavy bags.

At my ECG my doctor asked: what have they done to your heart?

Since taking your vitamin programme I am a different person. I am simply happy! My energy has returned and I can take stress again.

Also my back pains which I had suffered for years have totally disappeared! It is simply wonderful!

Yours sincerely,

Gisela Hölzler

Dear Dr. Rath,

I am 42 years old and have suffered from a **weak heart** since childhood. This made itself apparent through **difficulty breathing during exercise** such as climbing stairs, carrying heavy shopping bags etc and overall a chronic loss of efficiency. The constant lack of breath was however the most unbearable part.

Since May this year I have now been taking your Cellular Medicine formula, 1 tablet three times a day *Vitacor Plus, Enercor,* 1 tablet twice daily.

After eight weeks I was capable of much more. What was impressive was that I no longer need to stop when climbing stairs and my breathing normalises really quickly.

In conclusion I would like to say that I previously had a severely enlarged heart and my muscles were weak too. I am sure that I can achieve a better quality of life through taking your vitamin programme.

I hope you can help many other people with this.

Yours sincerely,

R.B.

Notes

6

Cardiac rhythm disorders (arrhythmia)

Dr Rath's Cellular Medicine Formula for prevention and basic therapy

Cardiac rhythm disorders – the breakthrough

Over 10 million people in Europe suffer from cardiac rhythm disorders (arrhythmia) caused by irregularities in the system for conveying electrical stimuli of the heart which is responsible for heartbeat. In most cases however, the causes of arrhythmia remained unknown until now. Arrhythmia with no known cause is so common that it is characterised by having its own diagnostic term: "paroxysmal arrhythmia".

Conventional orthodox medicine is also restricted simply to easing the symptoms. And so beta-blockers, calcium antagonists and other "anti-arrythmics" are prescribed.

In the case of cardiac rhythm disorders whereby there are long pauses between heartbeats, a pacemaker is implanted. In other cases attempt is made to "treat" the tissue of the cardiac muscle producing uncoordinated stimuli during a catheter examination and thus eradicate the core of the problem.

Modern Cellular Medicine now makes possible the breakthrough in researching the causes, prevention and causal treatment of this common disorder. The chief cause of cardiac rhythm disturbance is vitamin deficiency in millions of "electrical" cardiac muscles, which are responsible for the heart beating. A deficiency in vitamins and other constituents that are contained in Dr. Rath's vitamin programme leads to problems producing stimuli and conveying stimuli within the heart. The following letters vividly confirm this medical breakthrough.

Cellular Medicine and Cardiac Rhythm Disorder

<u>Principal cause:</u>
Vitamin deficiency
in millions of cells
of the cardiac muscle

<u>Prevention and
basic treatment</u>

Optimum supplement of
Dr. Rath's vitamin
programme, Principally:

- Vitamin C
- Magnesium
- Carnitine

Filling the cells
with biofuel

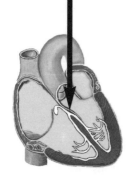

- Energy supply for
  electrical cardiac
  muscles
- Improved conduction
  of the stimuli respon-
  sible for heartbeat

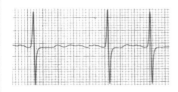

**Prevention and
basic therapy for
cardiac rhythm disorder**

Dear Dr. Rath,

In 1992 I suffered a **heart attack (posterior wall)** and since then **insufficiency of the left side of the heart (weak pumping efficiency of the left ventricle).** In November 1996 I chanced upon your book. Since my attack I had been studying specialist literature and also literature on dietetics. A change in diet brought mild relief from my complaints.

In spring 1995 I developed **cardiac rhythm disturbance** which was examined thoroughly in the hospital in Passau. Result: If it got worse, I must be treated with medicines or by treating the nerve cells in the heart. **The rhythm disturbance got worse with time. My physical performance was often reduced to below 70%.**
I didn't dare leave the house any more.

In November 1996, after studying your book, I immediately ordered your basic vitamin programme. After three weeks (9 tablets per day) the **cardiac rhythm disturbance had disappeared. It has never returned.**

After half a year even the breathing difficulties with exercise were gone.

Nitrospray was no longer necessary. Now after 18 months I can, at the age of 68, again go mountain walking. I also work in my business every day.

In the meantime I have completely lost faith in conventional medicine.

As a businessman I have really no objection to people wanting to make money. But it should **not be at the cost of someone else's health** as happens now with orthodox medicine.

Yours sincerely,

H.R.

Dear Dr. Rath,

I am 78 years old and have suffered for five years from cardiac rhythm disorders and also from diabetes for a year. Attacks of dizziness, physical debility, thrombosis and pulmonary embolisms in 1993 and 1997 were constantly with me as a result of my illness.

In July 1997 I was given a pacemaker, from which I suffered greatly. In June this year I began taking one tablet of your basic programme Vitacor Plus three times a day, and Enercor also from July, twice a day.

After only eight weeks my general condition was stable, I was more energetic and much more active. This was not the case before taking your Cellular Medicine formula. I could not even do work in the kitchen.

Now I am interested in everything again! On 24th August this year I had my blood checked. **The blood sugar level was okay!**

Another example of how well I am: also in August made a 14-day bus trip to the Tyrol. I mastered this with bravura, despite differences in altitude of 800 to 2800 m.

Despite the tremendous heat, 10-hour bus journey: **No difficulty breathing, no swollen legs and no problems with thrombosis!**

Yours sincerely,

Erika Walther

Dear Dr. Rath,

I am 67 years old and for around 25 to 30 years I have suffered acute heart problems. These problems manifested themselves in the form of **cardiac rhythm disturbance, angina pectoris, high blood pressure, breathing difficulties and heart pain.**

Through taking one tablet each of Vitacor Plus and Relacor three times daily and one tablet of Arteriforte once a day for five months I notice the following improvements in my state of health:

I hardly ever have cardiac rhythm disturbance, no difficulty breathing during exercise and have a much better sense of well-being. Also my blood pressure normalised, being now 135-140/80-85 in the mornings; previously it was 170/100.

As a result of this, I could take weaker medicines.

Furthermore, for many years I had suffered acute pain over my entire **spine.** Since taking your vitamin treatment **these symptoms too are as good as non-existent.**

I feel much more capable.

Yours sincerely,

Günter Seidler

Dear Dr. Rath,

In summer this year I learned of your vitamin programme. I have always been interested in natural therapy through my profession (chemist).

Since I was 19 I have suffered from disorders of the autonomic heart and circulatory system.

My husband has been suffering from cardiac rhythm disorders for over 20 years and has swallowed a great deal of medicine in that time, until in October last year a coronary vessel in and to his left ventricle almost completely closed up. The heart attack was a foregone conclusion!

We have both been taking *Vitacor Plus* and *Arteriforte* for two months. My husband takes one formula twice daily, whereas I take *Vitacor Plus* and *Arteriforte* twice as a precaution.

Result. **My husband had an ECG yesterday. No circulatory disorder could be detected and no more "irregularities " to be seen. Furthermore, his headaches had gone and the muscular cramp had disappeared.**

Although I take a somewhat smaller dose of the formula, I have noticed a significant increase in performance. There is neither tiredness nor exhaustion any longer.

It is a good thing that the results of your research have become more widely known and we can as a result experience an enormous improvement in the quality of life.

Yours sincerely,

Dagmar Schmidt

Dear Dr. Rath,

I am 76 years old and **have suffered from cardiac rhythm disturbance with racing of the heart** and other complaints for 20 years. There were often heavy palpitations also.

I have been taking 1 tablet three times a day from your basic vitamin programme since October 1996, then from January 1997 a double dose.

After nine months I no longer had any disease, my immune system is perfectly intact.

I don't go to the doctor any more as I no longer find it necessary. That says it all!

My three children and sons- and daughters-in-law take your basic treatment as a precaution.

Yours gratefully,

V.R.

Dear Dr. Rath,

I am 65 years old and for 12 years have been suffering the consequences of an obstruction in the right thigh and **from cardiac rhythm disturbance which amongst other things recorded as 1900 extra heartbeats during a long-term 24-hour ECG.** In addition seven years ago I developed **angina pectoris problems** and **blood pressure** gradually **rising to 185/95.**

The problems associated with this were kept under control by the regular taking of the medication "Lopirin Cor" and "Jenacard retard" prescribed by my GP.

But the rhythm disorders, more intense at night, frequently prevented me from sleeping normally and led, in conjunction with angina pectoris problems, to tiredness during the day, loss of performance and lack of drive.

In September last year I heard your lecture with great interest, read your books and since October have been a grateful user of your vitamin preparations. Initially I took six basic formula *Vitacor Plus* tablets daily, and since March this year three daily tablets of *Relacor,* one *Enercor* and one *Arteriforte.*

It has been possible meanwhile to halve the dosage of "Lopirin Cor".

After taking your preparations for about two months the night-time cardiac rhythm disturbance in particular reduced markedly, normal sleep was again possible and the daytime tiredness, loss in performance and lack of drive disappeared.

Now in August, after ten months, all that is left of the **angina pectoris complaints** is a slight burning sensation under the breastbone and I can speak of a healthy condition that I hadn't known in many years.

My GP was able to confirm this success, among other things, through a significantly improved ECG since March and blood pressure reduced to 168/77.

Many thanks,

Yours sincerely,

H. Schier.

Dear Dr. Rath,

I have been following your vitamin programme now for about one year and I have also noticed a great improvement in my health.

I am 43 years old and have always felt my **heart galloping from time to time, sometimes with a stabbing pain in the left-hand side of my heart.**

Both these symptoms have now disappeared completely and I feel considerably better. My dizzy spells have also become much less frequent.

I also used to suffer from problems with the connective tissue and for years my **haemorrhoids** used to cause me great discomfort with their pressure and pain. Creams used to bring only temporary relief. Since June 22nd this year I have been taking your additional formula *Arteriforte*. **After just one month, these annoying problems through haemorrhoids had disappeared completely,** although I still spend a lot of time sitting at my desk.

Now to the **circulation problems** in my legs. Here, too, symptoms such as stabbing pains, a dragging sensation and unpleasant pulsating sensations, especially in the left leg, have disappeared completely. I can even feel a pleasant tingling in my feet right down to my toes, and I can tell very clearly that the blood is circulating through my **feet** as they have become **nice and warm again, just like my hands.**

Yours sincerely,

Arnold Andreas Neumann

Dear Dr. Rath,

I am 45 years old and for five years I have suffered from an **irregular heartbeat.** Every time I did **physical work, no matter how minor,** my heartbeat became completely irregular. At work I was always suffering from a **loss of energy.**

For three months now I have been taking one tablet of your basic formula *Vitacor Plus* three times a day.

Already after three weeks I noticed that these feelings of exhaustion had become a thing of the past and that I had a lot more energy.

Even after physical exertion I no longer suffer from any signs of irregular heartbeat.

I have no trouble getting a good night's sleep, and at times when I used to be very prone to sinusitis, my health is now fully unimpaired.

Thank you!

Yours sincerely,

R. M.

Dear Dr. Rath,

I am 77 years old and have been **suffering for 18 years** from problems with an **irregular heartbeat.** Upon the slightest physical exertion I experienced **severe pains in the heart.** Most of all I had problems with my circulation. I have also had a heart attack.

Since February this year I have been taking your cellular medicine formulae *Vitacor Plus, Enercor* and *Arteriforte* in the following doses: *Vitacor Plus* three times a day 1 tablet, *Enercor* twice a day 1 tablet and *Arteriforte* once a day 1 tablet.

After three weeks the pains in my heart had almost disappeared. I also noticed that I could **breathe much more freely** and that the pains in my legs had subsided. I have informed my doctor of this improvement in my health.

As far as my general health is concerned, I am very satisfied and **am able to do many things that used to be impossible, such as gardening, housework and many other things.**

Yours sincerely,

Linda Neuber

Dear Dr. Rath,

I am 64 years old and for twelve years I have been suffering from **coronary pains** and high blood pressure, with sickness and an **irregular heartbeat.** I also used to suffer from feelings of anxiety.

Even after having my blood vessels dilated several times in the heart clinic at Bad Neustadt (1988-1992) I still didn't experience any real improvement. My feelings of nausea became more and more frequent, probably as a result of all the medication I was taking at the time - **Isoket retard, Adalat, Xanef, Godamet and beta-blockers. These had the additional side effects of causing bleeding in the gullet and fainting attacks.**

Since March 1st last year I have been taking your cellular medicine formulae.

After about three months I noticed that the times when I would suffer from irregularity of heartbeat were becoming much less frequent. **After eight months had elapsed these disturbances in rhythm had gone completely and my blood pressure had dropped to what has now become an average of 150/90.**

Gradually I have been able to leave off all my medication!

All my pains have vanished completely!

Yours sincerely,

E. M.

Dear Dr. Rath,

After my physical collapse in November 1996 I was admitted to Lukas Hospital in Altenkirchen. Doctors discovered I was suffering from **acute irregularities of the heartbeat and dysfunctional blood pressure and pulse.** After I had stopped taking medication, I was discharged with the recommendation that I undergo cardiac catheterisation. This was carried out in January 1997 at the University Clinic in Bonn. I was prescribed medication in the following doses: 1x Norvasc 5mg, 1x Aspirin 100, fi Bisaprolol 5, 1x Cranoc 20, 1x Isoket retard 20.

I was able to tolerate these medicines fairly well, but my **ability to work normally and to carry out usual tasks** was severely restricted.

In May 1997 I read your book. As a result, I began your vitamin course in June 1997.

Even after six months I was able to work better.

In the autumn of 1997 following my doctor's recommendation I attended a heart clinic for an examination of my heart. The results were so good that I was able to stop taking Isoket retard 20.

After a further examination by my own doctor in June 1998, all my body's readings were **back to normal.** Even my **blood pressure had returned to normal, 130 to 85/90 on average.**

Another exercise ECG examination was carried out. The doctors found that there were no heartbeat irregularities or thickening of the heart muscle.

When I mentioned your vitamin programme to the cardiologist, he said that he had heard about it and it was safe to assume that my good state of general health was a result of the cellular medicine formulae. He recommended that I carry on with your programme.

In closing, I must say that I am very pleased with the effectiveness of your vitamin programme and that I am sure it has done me good. I feel so well that I am now able to play football again. I have recommended your course of vitamins to two friends who also started taking your preparations and have meanwhile also noted an improvement in their health.

Yours sincerely,

Bernd Jung

Dear Dr. Rath,

I am 63 years old and have been suffering for six years from an **irregular pulse**. Once or twice every month I experienced **severe alterations in my heartbeat which would last from three to four hours.** It was the anxiety states that would sometimes make me **lose consciousness for several seconds** that caused me the most distress. On a few occasions I experienced panic attacks. In January this year it became so bad that I had to go into hospital.

The beta-blockers I was prescribed did me no good whatsoever, and my body did not respond to them at all well.

Since March this year I have been taking one tablet of *Vitacor Plus*, *Relacor* and *Metavicor* three times a day.

After four weeks I noticed that the irregularity in my heartbeat had gone altogether. I am now able to stand the heat and enjoy a glass of wine again from time to time.

I hope very much that many people will become interested in finding out about your Cellular Medicine, as from what I see around me and read about in the papers, half the world seems to be ill.

Best regards,

Renate Braun

Dear Dr. Rath,

For precisely four weeks now I have been taking your basic programme *Vitacor Plus* with *Arteriforte* and *Enercor.* I am 43 years old and as a self-employed person I am under a great deal of stress.

After about two weeks my irregular pulse started to become normal again, and after three weeks all symptoms had disappeared completely.

My mother has suffered a cerebral infarct, and I am pleased to be able to give her a vitamin course, too. I am keen to see if - and how - her condition will change for the better. What is certain is that during her course of traditional medical treatment my mother wasn't taking any additional vitamins.

Conventional medicine always tackles the symptoms and never the causes.

In these days of fast foods, I hope that many other people will realise just how important it is to take the right combination of vitamins.

Thank you!

Yours sincerely,

Thomas Funke

Dear Dr. Rath,

I started taking your basic formula and *Relacor* as no doctor, not even a super-specialist, has been able to diagnose the reasons for my high blood pressure which crops up from time to time. To start with, I was disappointed, as an instance of blood pressure had subsided just before I started with your programme.

I nevertheless began taking your two formulae, and to my astonishment I have to say that **after two weeks my irregular pulse had almost completely disappeared**, a chronic condition which according to heart specialists was non-pathological.

Beforehand, my heart would skip a beat between **three and ten times a minute**. After these two weeks, I am lucky if it skips a beat **once every minute**, in other words it is behaving quite normally.

Yours sincerely,

M. L.

Dear Dr. Rath,

I am 70 years old and for ten years I have been suffering from a **rapid pulse**. One of my heart valves is calcified, and I suffer from occasional **pains in the heart.** I also suffer from shortness of breath when climbing stairs.

I have been taking beta-blockers for many years (medication to lower the blood pressure). This medication has a bad effect on me - my hair falls out, I suffer from nightmares, and I often have hallucinations and flickering in front of the eyes.

Since July this year I have been taking one tablet of your basic formula *Vitacor Plus* three times a day.

After four to five weeks I can say that my shortness of breath has become considerably better and the pains in my heart have almost gone.

Yours sincerely,

G. S.

Dear Dr. Rath,

I am a 75-year old woman and I am very glad and grateful that I have discovered your cellular medicine programme, as these **vitamins have given** me **new energy**. I seize every opportunity I can to tell others about my positive experience.

I suffered from high blood pressure, going up to more than 200, irregular pulse, weakness of the heart and high cholesterol levels.

After I had suffered a slight **heart attack** in June last year I had an operation on the left-side carotid artery. In November doctors discovered **that my right carotid artery was also almost closed up and would soon have to be operated on.**

However, after I had been taking your vitamins for four months, **my surgeon carried out an ultrasonic examination and found that my arteries are now completely clear.**

My blood pressure is back to normal, my irregular pulse is back to normal, and I feel just like I used to years ago.

I used to have to take nine traditional medicine tablets per day; nowadays I take just four.

Before I started taking the vitamins, I tried talking about your treatment with my **doctor,** but she just wouldn't hear of it. But after she had **received the positive report written by my surgeon she was quite amazed** and has started reading your book "Why Animals Don't Get Heart Attacks" and listening to your Chemnitz cassette with great interest.

I can only repeat that I have derived enormous benefit from the vitamins and would like to thank you once again for this result.

When I was really feeling at my lowest, I took 2 tablets of the basic formula every day, for four weeks. At the moment I am taking 1 *Vitacor Plus,* 1 *Relacor,* 1 *Enercor* and 1 *Metavicor* a day.

Many thanks to you for your research work!

Yours sincerely,

F. M.

Dear Dr. Rath,

I am 46 years old. Four years ago I had a kidney transplant and in April 1996 a heart attack. I have been taking *Vitacor Plus* for one year now, two tablets a day.

After just four weeks I was starting to feel better in myself, and the massive problems I had with my irregular heartbeat disappeared almost immediately.

Yours sincerely,

M. Müller

7

Diabetes
and diabetic circulatory
problems

**Dr. Rath's
Cellular Medicine programme
for natural prevention
and basic therapy**

Diabetes - the medical breakthrough

Millions of Europeans suffer from diabetes-related metabolic disorders. In Germany alone there are more than one million diabetics. Heart attacks, strokes and other circulatory disorders are some of the feared consequences of diabetes. There are two types of diabetes: the form that people are born with (Type I) and the form that people acquire (Type II): the second form occurs most commonly in adulthood. Type I diabetes is usually caused by an inherent deficiency in the body's ability to produce insulin in the pancreas. The causes of metabolic dysfunction in adults on the other hand are largely unknown, which is the reason for the worldwide spread of this illness.

Conventional medicine is restricted to treating the symptoms of diabetes, that is to say to lowering the blood sugar level. But even if this level is well adjusted, cardiac and circulatory conditions still frequently occur. Lowering the blood sugar level is an essential factor in treating diabetes, but on its own it is not sufficient. Without knowing what the factors are which cause diabetes, an effective prevention and treatment of diabetes is not possible.

Modern Cellular Medicine has brought about a real breakthrough in research into the causes, prevention and supportive treatment of adult diabetes. Altered diabetic metabolism is usually caused by a chronic deficiency in vitamins and other cell-related factors in millions of cells in the insulin-producing pancreas and in the artery wall.

The following letters received from diabetics emphatically confirm this medical breakthrough. Cellular Medicine therefore helps to eradicate this common disease as well.

Diabetes-related cardiac and circulatory disorders

<u>Principal cause:</u>
Vitamin deficiency
in millions of cells
of the

Arterial
wall   Pancreas

<u>Prevention and
basic treatment</u>

Optimal supplement of
Dr. Rath's vitamin
programme, chiefly:

- Vitamin C
- Vitamin E
- chromium

Filling the cells with
bio-fuel

- Regulation of the
  body's insulin
  balance
- Repair of the arte-
  rial wall

**Prevention and basic treatment
of diabetic complications such
as**
- **heart attack**
- **strokes**
- **kidney failure**
- **blindness**
- **gangrene**

Dear Dr. Rath,

I am 42 years of age and have had **diabetes for two years now.** The effects are tiredness, thirst and glucose in the urine. Most of all I have suffered from **a lack of vitality.**

Since May this year I have been taking *Vitacor Plus* (3 x 1) and *Diacor* (2 x 1). **After just two weeks my blood sugar level was** so **normal** that I feel completely well without taking Manninil.

It is the improvement in my general health which has pleased me most of all.

My **doctor confirmed this improvement** when he measured a constant normalisation of my blood sugar level.

Yours sincerely,

R. W.

Dear Dr. Rath,

I am 75 years old and have been a diabetic for many years. About one year ago my **blood sugar level** went up enormously. It **fluctuated between 15 and 17 mmol/l (270 - 305 mg/dl).** The doctor who was treating me wanted me to change over to insulin injections, but I did not want that.

I began taking the food supplement *Diacor* in combination with *Vitacor Plus.* It was still possible for me to switch over to insulin injections at any time should there not be an improvement in my blood sugar levels.

However, I hardly dared believe that **after just a short time** of regularly taking *Diacor* and *Vitacor Plus* (2 tablets a day of each) and neural treatment from a non-medical practitioner, **my blood sugar level had dropped. It now fluctuates between 6.5 and 9.5 mmol/l (117 to 171).** But if that weren't enough, my **whole well-being** has improved enormously. You can imagine how happy I am about this, as **it means I don't have to have injections.**

I am extremely happy with my current general health. I would be very pleased if many other people suffering from diabetes were able to improve their health problems with this vitamin programme, or even be completely cured.

Yours sincerely,

H. S.

Dear Dr. Rath,

I am 69 years old and have been suffering from **high blood pressure for 20 years. For three years I have also been suffering from diabetes.** During this time I have suffered from symptoms which have increased as time has gone on, such as general tiredness and lack of interest, and stiff joints. Latterly I suffered from **cold and numb toes.**

Since 25th June this year I have been taking one tablet of your basic formula *Vitacor Plus* and one tablet of your restorative formula *Relacor* three times a day.

After only three weeks the feeling came back in my toes and my feet and they felt warm again.

I have also become more supple again, and I can do jobs I'm not used to doing without any difficulty or pain.

I am fit again; **it's been a long while since I felt as well as I do now!**

Yours sincerely,

Klaus Schumacher

Dear Dr. Rath,

I am 60 years old and have suffered from **diabetes for six years.** My symptoms have been **difficulties in seeing properly, scurfy patches on my skin, bleeding gums, tiredness and thirst.** It was feeling tired during the day that was the most unpleasant for me.

Since May last year I have been taking your Cellular Medicine formulae, 1 tablet three times a day of *Vitacor Plus* and 1 *Diacor* tablet.

After three weeks I regained my full sight, and my other symptoms have nearly all disappeared.

I hope a lot of people will get to hear about this course of vitamins. I will do my bit to that end.

Yours sincerely,

Jürgen Schäfer

Dear Dr. Rath,

I am 75 years old. As well as having **diabetes**, a year ago I suffered a stroke. But the worst problem for me was **poor circulations in my legs.**

For four weeks now I have been taking your Cellular Medicine formulae, three times a day I take 3 tablets of *Vitacor Plus* and 1 tablet of *Diacor* and 1 of *Arteriforte*.

After this period of time I can say that **the circulation in my legs has improved and that my blood sugar levels have gone down to 100-113 mg/dl.**

When he saw this improvement in my health, my **doctor was lost for words,** especially as he had already been considering the possibility of **amputating my legs.**

I can do light housework again, such as ironing and cooking.

I owe this to my daughter, Ute Heinz, and friends; it was they who introduced me to your vitamin programme and made me enjoy life again.

Yours sincerely,

Edeltraud Heinz

Dear Dr. Rath,

Studying your book led me to thoroughly re-think my health situation. I have always been interested in medical problems, but now I have been thinking about these things in a new intensity and depth - as far as a technical person is able to understand medicine.

I am 67 years old and suffer from hereditary diabetes mellitus, heart problems and weak arteries. I have doctors' certificates attesting the following illnesses:

- **diabetes mellitus with complications** (1970 diabetes manifest, discovered by my dentist as a result of severe bleeding of the gums and parodontitis, **four operations on my gums - it was the beginning of scurvy!**)

- cerebro-vascular deficiency (inadequate circulation of blood in the brain)

- reduced heart output with coronary cardiopathy and **high blood pressure** (1976-1990 increased levels of up to 180/100; 1990/91 **heart attacks**, 1994 treatment by a heart specialist with 75 mg Atenolol, 40 mg Mifedipin, 10 mg ACE inhibitors, 100 mg AS5 per day and in emergencies Nitro-Spray, 1996 extreme loss of vitality)

- constantly **swollen ankles and lower legs,** fluid on both my shins, the first open places for six weeks, in 1997 my blood pressure fell to 90/58 with a pulse of 49,

- **peripheral circulatory disorders** (in the limbs),

- Although I am very careful about what I eat (I am almost a vegetarian), have lost nine kilos and weigh just one kilo more than my ideal weight, I have very high **cholesterol levels, from 190 to 250 mg/dl.**

In addition to these problems, I also suffered from **neuropathic dysfunction (damage to the nerves) in my feet, with severe numbness** - I no longer had any feeling when pricked with a drawing pin - and loss of balance and what is sometimes called „window-shopping legs" with frequent cramps and pains in my legs and feet. Occasionally I suffered from autonomous nervous disorders.

After I had been taking vitamins since February this year, following the advice given in your book, I learned in May about the health network and the sale of your formulae. I started working in the network immediately and am currently taking three tablets of *Vitacor Plus,* three tablets of *Diacor* and four tablets of *Arteriforte* every day

I have been taking the cellular medicine formula for six months now and can report the following:

- In cooperation with my doctor I have been able to stop taking all the calcium antagonists, the beta-blockers, ACE inhibitors and AS 5, as well as the diuretics. I am still taking 16 mg of a Ansiotensin II receptor blockers and 100 mg of Pentoxifyllin.

- The pains and cramps in my legs have disappeared and the first signs of feeling are starting to come back in my feet, tests with a microfilament give positive results at four places. I have sensations on the soles of my feet again when I am tickled there, but I still have some pain.

- the autonomous neuropathies have receded. I am able to walk around town again without first having to plan toilet stops.

- My physical strength has increased considerably. **In January I needed to stop six to eight times in order to walk up a 200 m path with a 13% slope; now I can complete the distance briskly without having to stop at all.** It used to take me 65 minutes in January to complete a distance on the flat; now I can complete the distance in 45 minutes.

- As for the diabetes treatment, I had the option of leaving off either 5 mg of **Glibenclamid or 10 units of prolonged action insulin.** I decided to leave off the tablet.

- All the measures I was taking to combat my high cholesterol level have allowed me to leave off the **cholesterol depressants.** My doctor was pleased with this development, too.

- The **pulses in my feet** have been clearly evident again for about six weeks now; this is an enormous step forward for me.

I am firmly resolved to continue this course of treatment I have begun. I shall put the motto "Patience is the key to joy" up on the wall. I shall report back to you again in a few months' time.

With my sincerest thanks and best wishes,

Yours,

Dr. K. G. W.

Dear Dr. Rath,

Since May this year I have been taking your preparations and have met with great success.

In 1997 I suffered a slight stroke and have as a result had to undergo an operation to the carotid artery.

Since 1984 I am registered as a **category II diabetic.**

In the past few months, the HBA 1 value (the laboratory test for the mean **blood sugar level** taken over the last 2-3 weeks) has gone down considerably from 9.6 to 6.2.

The circulation in my legs and feet has also improved visibly. On the whole, I am able to walk much better.

Kind regards,

W. B.

Dear Dr. Rath,

I am 56 years old and have suffered from diabetes for ten years. My blood sugar count was measured at **between 9.0 and 14.0 mmol/l (160 to 250 mg/dl).**

Since January this year I have been taking one tablet of *Vitacor Plus* and one tablet of *Diacor* mornings and evenings. My blood sugar count is now between **4.0 and 8.0 mmol/l (70 to 140 mg/dl).**

With my doctor's approval, I have been able to reduce the medicines I was taking to treat the diabetes.

Yours sincerely,

Egon Stölzel

Dear Dr. Rath,

For two weeks now I have been taking *Arteriforte* and *Diacor* regularly.

I no longer suffer from **cramps in the feet,** the continuous twitching has stopped, and beforehand I was unable to keep my right foot still because of the continuous pain day and night.

When I began taking your preparations, the sugar count went up slightly; it then went down considerably.

Yours sincerely,

F. K.

Dear Dr. Rath,

I am 58 years of age and have suffered for about five years from the **late symptoms of diabetes: loss of sight, circulatory disorders with diabetic gangrene in the feet** (they told me they might have to consider amputation), **high blood pressure,** serious heart problems, very poor renal values.

After I had heard a report on Bavarian radio, I immediately went out and bought your book.

For about two years now I have been taking 2 tablets from your vitamin programme three times a day. After about twelve months I noticed the following improvement in my general state of health:

- **constant blood pressure,**

- **improved renal values (as a result, I was able to avoid having to undergo dialysis treatment just in the nick of time),**

- **what was particularly noticeable was that my feet almost completely healed, with the prevention of what looked like unavoidable amputation of my legs.**

My positive experiences mean that I am able to recommend your vitamin programme to other people without the slightest reservation.

Yours sincerely,

Walter Habermann

Dear Dr. Rath,

I have been a diabetic for more than 40 years now. After treatment with a high dosage of *Diacor* I am able to see the first positive results.

I feel fit and well and note **an improvement in my polyneuropathy** (polyneuropathy is damage to the nerves, typical for diabetics; it can lead to a lack of feeling and numbness, especially in the legs).

I was in danger of losing a toe on my right foot - and yesterday my doctor found that the condition had improved.

I am pleased to be able to tell you that your vitamin programme has enabled me to combat the diabetes and improve my general state of health.

Thank you very much.

Yours sincerely,

E. B.

Dear Dr. Rath,

I would like to start off by thanking you from the bottom of my heart for your work.

I am 76 years old and have suffered from **diabetes** since 1977. My GP has treated me with tablets over many years. In the course of the years, my feet and **legs and lower legs turned nearly dark blue.**

In 1991 I was **paralysed down the left side of my face.** My left eye, left nostril and the left part of my lower lip were most affected by the **damage caused to my nerves.**

I have been taking your course of vitamins since March of this year. I take 6 tablets a day of your basic programme *Vitacor Plus* and 6 *Diacor* tablets a day.

My condition improved after just eight weeks. At the present moment in time I can report the following:

1. **It is now impossible to detect the damage to my left eye.** My eyelid does not droop anymore, and the feeling of having a completely dry eye has all but gone.

2. The symptoms of the damage caused to my lower lip were a continuous feeling of **dryness and numbness.** Both these symptoms have **disappeared completely.**

3. The left part of my **nose** was always dry and I had no feeling in it. Today, everything is back to **normal again.**

4. I had serious problems with the **circulation in my lower legs and feet.** I always suffered from cold feet. Dark patches had start to form on the insides of my ankles because my feet were not getting enough blood.

Today, **my feet are warm again and my circulation is normal.** The dark patches on my left foot have become a bit paler; on my right foot the patches have become a lot paler.

5. My **daily blood sugar count** (measured with rods and blood) **is almost normal again.**

I can hardly tell you how grateful I am. Thanks to your preparations I am able to enjoy a good quality of life again. I am greatly encouraged.

The only thing I really regret is that I did not find out about your vitamin programme until now, now that I am in old age. I am quite convinced that my problems could have been avoided if I had known about your vitamins earlier.

I can warmly recommend anyone who is suffering from diabetes to begin taking your course as soon as possible. I have told all my friends, neighbours, and all the doctors and chemists I know about your treatment. I have also passed the books and other material I have on for other people to read.

My hope for millions of other people is that they hear about your vitamin programme as soon as possible so that illnesses can be prevented and suffering reduced.

I wish you lots of energy for your continued work. I hope that one day you will have the success you deserve with your admirable work.

Again, thank you very much.

Yours sincerely,

W. G.

Dear Dr. Rath,

I have been a category II diabetic for 16 years now and have been injecting myself with insulin for 14 years. Before I started following your cellular medicine vitamin programme, I was an ill-adjustable diabetic.

My blood sugar count was very high, fluctuating between good and bad. At the time, my long-term HbA 1c value was 8.4.

In March this year I began taking your *Vitacor Plus* and *Diacor* tablets, one tablet of each twice a day.

Not only did my metabolic process start to stabilise, but I even managed to achieve **optimal values.** There is no doubt about this whatsoever; we only need to refer to my **blood sugar count!** My current HbA 1c long-term value is 6.6.

I have also been able to reduce my intake of insulin by about one third. In the course of time, one of the added benefits of this will be the saving in cost to my health insurance company.

Although I can be classed as an intensive user of insulin, taking the new 'Humalog' drug, I maintain that your vitamin programme has contributed to the improvement in my blood sugar levels and to the overall improvement in my general state of health.

I shall continue taking your Cellular Medicine formulae together with the insulin. On the strength of my positive experiences I can recommend it to all diabetics who might be interested.

Yours sincerely,

Günter Behm

Notes

8

Dr. Rath's Cellular Medicine Formulae for the prevention and basic treatment of other common illnesses:

- varicose veins

- asthma

- skin disorders

- eye diseases

- headaches

- others

VARICOSE VEINS

Dear Dr. Rath,

I am 42 years old and have been suffering from **varicose veins for six years.** I have been continuously plagued by severe pains in the legs and **cramp in my calf muscles** at night.

Four months ago I began taking *Vitacor Plus* and *Arteriforte* regularly. **After just eight weeks the night-time attacks of cramp had become a thing of the past** and I was even able to walk and stand for longer periods of time without experiencing any pain.

I am immensely impressed by your vitamin programme and have already recommended it to many others.

Yours sincerely,

Gabriele Winkler

Dear Dr. Rath,

For about five weeks now I have been taking the following products: *Femiforte, Vitacor, Arteriforte* and *Metavicor.*

Metavicor: Improved digestion, cholesterol greatly reduced to normal levels.

Arteriforte: Improved circulation, left foot lets me sleep at night without bothering me; before, I was always in pain from my varicose veins. Now, my varicose **veins are receding**, and I am free of pain.

My nerves are better, and my general health has improved considerably.

Because of these fantastic results, I can warmly recommend the products made by Dr. Rath that I have listed above; in fact, this is something that I do very actively.

Yours sincerely,

B. K.

Dear Dr. Rath,

I have been talking *Vitacor Plus, Arteriforte* and *Femicell* regularly for eight weeks now.

Arteriforte: I have suffered for several years from internal **varicose veins** and have already undergone an operation for them (about 10 years ago). However, varicose veins occurred again at the same spot. At times they were so sensitive that even a blanket over my feet caused me severe pain.

Just three days after I had been begun taking Arteriforte I noticed a considerable improvement in sensitivity, and after one week I was free of pain.

Femicell: Even during my first period after I had begun taking *Femicell* I no longer suffered from **period pains** (beforehand I used to have a dragging sensation in my lower abdomen and backache).

Yours sincerely,

B. K.

Dear Dr. Rath,

I am 37 years old and have suffered from **swollen legs** for four years. After I had had an inflamed wound, my leg was red with scars and swollen through an **accumulation of fluid.** Standing and walking caused me the most pain.

In March this year I began taking 1 *Vitacor Plus* tablet three times a day and 1 *Arteriforte* tablet once a day; after two months I began to notice an improvement in my health.

The swellings on my legs have **almost completely disappeared** and the scars and patches have become smaller, too.

Even my varicose veins are receding. I hope I will be able to tell many more people about the effect of your Cellular Medicine formulae.

Yours sincerely,

B. G.

ASTHMA

Dear Dr. Rath,

I am 62 years old and have been suffering from **bronchial asthma** for 25 years, together with colds (neglected flu). Most of all I have been suffering from **asthma attacks** and attendant **shortness of breath.**

Since April of this year I have been taking your Cellular Medicine formulae: 3 *Vitacor Plus* tablets daily and 3 *Relacor* tablets three times daily.

After eleven weeks I no longer had to use my spray, which beforehand had been my constant companion. I was able to breathe freely once again.

This is the best thing that could possibly happen to me!

Yours sincerely,

Marianne Stein

Dear Dr. Rath,

I was born in 1924 and until I reached the age of 60 I was bothered by few health problems. Then I became very ill, and the doctors diagnosed life-threatening **anaemia** and **asthma**. Despite many examinations, the cause for my anaemia could not be determined. For almost ten years I had to receive one or two blood transfusions a year. Although the haemoglobin value had improved during the last three years, it still went up and down a lot.

I often suffered tremendous **shortness of breath as a result of the asthma.**

Since the beginning of the year I have been taking your Cellular Medicine formulae: *Vitacor Plus* basic formula, *Enercor* and *Femiforte*.

Over the last few weeks I have noticed a **clear improvement in my health** and I am very pleased that my blood readings taken in April and on August 22nd this year show very good, stable values.

My asthma has improved too.

Best regards,

Gudrun Heumann

Dear Dr. Rath,

I am 56 years old and have suffered from **bronchial asthma** for almost ten years. The illness began with a flu-type infection with severe bronchitis for which my GP prescribed "Allergospasmin" inhaler (a medicine in spray form designed to resolve the spasms of the small air cells in the lungs).

Since then, I was **unable to leave the house,** sometimes not even the room, **without having this medicine with me.** On good days, I needed to inhale it "only" every three to seven hours. Whenever I had a flu-type infection, I often needed to use it every one to one-and-a-half hours, day and night. **I was often on the verge of suffocating.**

I have tried all sorts of treatments, both alternative natural methods and antibiotics, cortisone and anti-allergic agents. Nothing was really able to help. As I could almost set my watch by the length of time between the shortness of breath attacks, I had long been convinced that I had developed a medication dependency.

For three months (i.e. since June 2nd this year) I have been taking your Cellular Medicine formulae, *Vitacor Plus* (3x daily 1 tbl.), *Relacor* (3x daily 1 tbl.) and *Femiforte* (1 tbl. daily).

After four weeks, I started to lengthen the time between my aerosol inhalations. It was a real withdrawal for me and more or less a torture, but it got better and better.

One whole week passed before the last time I had to inhale, and that's now two months ago. Occasionally I would still suffer some shortness of breath, but I stuck it out, and from day to day these attacks became less bothersome and more infrequent. My suspicion that I had had for years, that a weak heart and irregularity of the heartbeat were the basic causes of my asthma, was confirmed; these had receded into the background because of the relaxing effect of the asthma preparations.

Since January I have also been taking *Enercor* and *Arteriforte* and my **recovery is progressing by leaps and bounds.**

I still can't believe that shortness of breath and medicine dependency are things of the past.

This is a new life for me! Thank you, Dr. Rath!

Yours sincerely,

Doris Hildebrandt

Dear Dr. Rath,

For many years I used to suffer from recurrent infections. I often had bronchitis twice a year. About three years ago this took the form of **spastic bronchitis**.

Since the beginning of the year I have been taking *Vitacor Plus* and *Femiforte* from your vitamin programme, and since about April I have also been taking *Arteriforte.* This very quickly led to a solid overall improvement in my general health. **My susceptibility to infections has practically disappeared,** and I am able to cope much better with stress.

Since listening to your cassette "Basics of Cellular Medicine", I have also been taking your additional formula *Relacor,* taking between one and two tablets a day.

There has since been a noticeable change in my **lungs.** Everything has become much **clearer, and I am able to draw really deep breaths.**

Thank you very much indeed once again for all that you have done!

With best regards,

Gerda Tecklenburg

Dear Dr. Rath,

I have been suffering from **asthma** for many years, more so since 1981. In 1996 I was admitted to hospital three times with a suspected heart attack. Fortunately, this was never confirmed! The pains always began on the left side beneath the last rib, accompanied by shortness of breath. Through dedicated care and the use of the latest technology together with all types of medication, I was able to leave hospital on each occasion. I was given **oxygen equipment,** and this helped me to accomplish my everyday household chores.

I am also suffering from a build up of fluid in the legs. At Dresden Heart Clinic my daily intake of fluid was set at 1.5 litres. But the water still remained in my legs.

It was only on the recommendation of a non-medical practitioner who was treating me that I have started taking your *Vitacor Plus, Enercor* and *Relacor* that **the swellings in my legs have gone down enormously;** when the weather is cooler the swellings often disappear altogether.

At the same time my general health has improved. I have been able to manage for **weeks now without inhalations.** A trip into the hills climbing up 100 metres is no problem for me at all, and at home I am no longer afraid to climb two floors to go into the loft.

This is a marvellous success after only six months!

Yours sincerely,

J. N.

SKIN / PSORIASIS / ALLERGIES

Dear Dr. Rath,

I have been working in your network since January this year. For 22 years I have suffered from **psoriasis** and have been under the treatment of dermatologists.

In February I heard about your lectures. At that time I had psoriasis the **size of the palm of a hand**, on both elbows, on both knees and on my head. I sought the help of a nutritional advisor in your network. She recommended I take a zinc preparation together with *Vitacor Plus*. I followed her advice and started taking the zinc preparation, one capsule mornings and evenings. Shortly afterwards I began taking *Vitacor Plus,* one tablet in the morning, at midday and in the evening.

It is now October, and with the exception of a tiny spot on my scalp I have been free of this bothersome complaint for about two weeks now. **My arms and legs are smooth again, as if they had never had anything wrong with them.** I would therefore like to take this opportunity to thank you, Dr. Rath, and your advisor, for your help. As I know there are many people suffering from this disease, I would like for them, too, to learn about your wonderful method. I am therefore quite happy for you to publish my letter.

Yours sincerely,

Wolfgang Horn

Dear Dr. Rath,

I am 51 years of age. I have suffered for 30 years from a **pollen allergy** that begins every year in April and goes away again sometime in July. Frequent **flu-type infections** and difficulty in breathing are always a continuous torture for me during this time. I also used to suffer from bad backache.

Since December last year I have been taking your cellular medicine formulae, one *Vitacor Plus* tablet three times a day and one *Femiforte* tablet three times a day. After five months I have noticed the following improvements in my general health:

I no longer have any **infections** and **my allergy was nowhere near as bad as in previous years.** I am also very pleased that my backache has been reduced to a minimum.

And there's something else, too. Since my operation for the removal of my womb at the age of 38, I had continuously to take **hormone preparations.** When I began your course of vitamin treatment, I was able to **leave off this medication.**

I feel very well!

Yours sincerely,

Helga Irmler

Dear Dr. Rath,

For three years my husband, aged 73, suffered from an allergy in **the neck, shoulder and face region.** He also suffered from circulatory problems in his right leg. No doctor was really able to bring him any relief.

On July 10th this year my husband started taking *Vitacor Plus,* one tablet three times a day. After just one week the itching disappeared and his nerves calmed down. Two weeks later, three quarters of his allergy had vanished. After a total of just four weeks all that my husband had was a lymph swelling on his neck.

After four weeks he started taking *Arteriforte* as well, one tablet twice a day, and after another month he began taking Metavicor, one tablet three times a day.

The itching has gone, the allergy has gone and the circulatory problems have almost disappeared, too. My husband is his happy, jolly self again, just like he used to be before his illness.

I also had problems with high blood pressure and slight arteriosclerosis (I am 60 years of age). **My blood pressure was 200/100.** I also started taking *Vitacor Plus* on July 10th this year, just like my husband, and in the same dose.

After fourteen days my blood pressure had improved. **A month later it had become normal, after a course of *Relacor*.** It had become normal again after another month. I feel healthy and strengthened. Through taking *Arteriforte* and *Femiforte* my knee and finger joints have become more supple and free of pain.

Thank you very much indeed. We tell everyone we meet everywhere about your cellular medicine formulae.

I have been a nurse for 35 years and have never before seen such results, only the misery that results from conventional medicine!

Thank you very much once again.

Yours sincerely,

Anna-Sibylla Saatz

ARTHROSIS / OSTEOPOROSIS

Dear Dr. Rath,

My mother, Mrs. Maria Kohlmann, has experienced great success with *Vitacor Plus*. She is 75 years of age and suffers from **rheumatism**. She has pains mostly in the arms. When she tries lifting her arms it causes her great pain.

For one year she took a **cortisone preparation** prescribed by the doctor. Sometimes the medication would help to ease the pain, but she was never really free of pain.

Finally I was able to persuade her to try Dr. Rath's *Vitacor Plus*. After about two months she reduced the amount of cortisone she was still taking as the pains had subsided considerably.

One month later she was beaming with joy as she told me how she could **move her arms again as normal, and that the pain had disappeared completely.**

She has now stopped taking cortisone completely.

Yours sincerely,

Maria Kohlmann and Rosemarie Brandl

Dear Dr. Rath,

These are the complaints I had before I started taking your Cellular Medicine formulae:

1. **Severe hair loss for weeks on end**; nothing that I did could stop it.

2. **Arthritis and back pains for many years** following an operation for a slipped disc. Because of this I had to use **two crutches wherever I went** at all times. Standing caused me tremendous pain and I was unable to do any housework.

3. As a result of thrombosis and cardiac insufficiency **my feet were swollen** in the evenings, despite wearing support stockings.

After I started taking your Cellular Medicine formulae *Vitacor Plus* and *Enercor* I noticed the following improvements in my general health:

1. After 3 days **my hair loss disappeared altogether.**

2. I am now able to work around the house **without crutches.** I am able to cook again and use both hands to carry things with. I am also able to do light housework.

3. **My legs are slim** and my shoes fit me better.

Thank you very much,

Sincerely yours,

L. D.

Dear Dr. Rath,

I am 55 years old and have suffered for 14 years from **osteoporosis.** Since I had a radical hysterectomy (removal of the womb) 14 years ago I have suffered from unbearable **backache and pains in the bones.** My bodily posture has changed and I have become smaller.

After I had had broken bones on several occasions (comminuted fractures), the doctors diagnosed osteoporosis. I was continuously afraid of breaking bones again.

Since April this year I have been taking your Cellular Medicine formulae *Vitacor Plus* and *Femiforte,* 1 tablet three times a day.

After four months my health had improved and I was free of all pain. The fact that I am almost able to walk upright again is an enormous change. This improvement in my health has been confirmed by **new X-rays; they show that the osteoporosis has disappeared.**

I shall do my bit to spread the word about your vital information on vitamin research and Cellular Medicine, so that other people may be helped.

Yours sincerely,

Christine Ralle

Dear Dr. Rath,

I am 55 years old and for 10 years I have been suffering from **arthritis of the fingers.** This complaint causes a gradual **stiffening of the hands.** The recurring inflammation has given me an awful amount of pain.

In 1996 I began following your basic vitamin course, taking 1 tablet three times a day.

After 18 months I can safely say: **The pains have subsided, and above all, the times when my finger joints become inflamed are** far less frequent. My doctor has also recommended I continue taking your vitamins.

Yours sincerely,

H. J.

Dear Dr. Rath,

I am 58 years of age and have been suffering from osteoporosis for eight years. My symptoms were severe backache and pains in the joints, like a bad case of flu. I also suffered from pains in the lower abdomen.

For six weeks I have been taking *Vitacor Plus* and *Femiforte* from your Cellular Medicine formulae programme,1 tablet three times a day. After three weeks my backache had reduced considerably, and the bleeding between periods stopped.

I have also been taking oestrogen for 16 years (prescribed by various gynaecologists). My doctor has agreed for me to stop taking this, and I feel very well with Dr. Rath's vitamin programme.

Yours sincerely,

B. W.

Dear Dr. Rath,

I am 48 years old and have had to take **oestrogen** for the last two years following a **radical hysterectomy** in 1996. Hot flushes and **the start of osteoporosis in the neck region** (quite clearly visible in X-rays) were a real burden for me.

In January this year I began taking *Vitacor Plus* and *Femiforte* from your vitamin programme, 1 tablet three times a day.

After about two months the annoying **hot flushes had stopped** and **the pains around my neck vertebrae** had subsided considerably. I also notice that I have much more energy.

In February I was able to stop taking the **oestrogen** and have been able to achieve far better results with your Cellular Medicine formulae than with the hormone replacement therapy.

Yours sincerely,

Petra Bollmohr

EYE DISEASES

Dear Dr. Rath,

About one year ago I recommended my aunt (65) in Nuremberg to try your vitamin programme. She was sceptical and refused to consider it, having heard negative reports about it. She said she was already eating a lot of fruit and took vitamin tablets from to time.

I told her that that was not enough, and I was finally able to convince her to try out your basic vitamin programme, 3 x 1 tablet a day.

After about one month she phoned me to say her galloping heartbeat had completely gone. She was over the moon.

She also told me of the general improvement in her state of health. She had more energy and did not get so easily out of breath when jogging, like she used to do.

Before she started with the course of vitamins, her optician had diagnosed a **considerable worsening of her eye condition.** He asked her to go back for another eye examination six months later.

After a half a year on the vitamin programme she went back to have her eyes tested. The doctor was amazed and said her **eyes had improved considerably.** She asked him: Doctor, how is that possible? He was lost for an answer.

Six months later she had her eyes tested again. The doctor confirmed that the **internal pressure in the eye had become normal,** and her sight had improved, too.

She revealed her secret of Dr. Rath's vitamin programme and said she was absolutely delighted.

Today, she is a staunch defender of your vitamin programme. She feels fit and well and would never want to be without your tablets again.

Yours sincerely,

Arnold H. Neumann

HEADACHE / MIGRAINE

Dear Dr. Rath,

I am 47 years old and have suffered for 22 years from migraine. Through a paralysis of the facial nerve on the right side of my face I have suffered from **severe headaches just above my right eye** since 1977. I have also suffered many times from trigeminus neuralgia. I have sought the help of many doctors, but a lasting improvement has not been possible, merely a temporary reduction in the pain.

Since March this year I have been taking one tablet of your basic formula *Vitacor Plus* three times a day, and since July I have also been taking one *Arteriforte* tablet three times a day.

After about two weeks I was experiencing periods when I was completely free of pain. The slight pains I was now having were quite bearable in comparison with what I had been used to earlier. My quality of life has improved considerably. I am able to perform tasks and do not get exhausted so quickly as before.

After all those years there were times when I just felt like giving up. But all that has changed now!

Yours sincerely,

S. S.

Dear Dr. Rath,

I am 24 years of age and have been suffering from headaches for six years. **Severe headache** would develop every time after I had indulged in heavy physical exercise and after long periods of work.

Since June this year I have been taking your Cellular Medicine formulae *Vitacor Plus* and *Relacor,* one tablet of each three times a day.

After eight weeks I noticed that **my headaches had become very rare.** What is especially noticeable was that when I do get headaches, they are very slight indeed.

Taking your course of vitamins has vastly improved my quality of life. I am able to do a lot more! Thank you, Dr. Rath. I hope you will be able to help many people just like you have been able to help me.

Yours sincerely,

A. G.

[page 212]

Dear Dr. Rath,

I am 77 years of age and for many years I have suffered from **circulatory disorders** accompanied by **headaches and dizzy spells** which often prevent me from walking just a few steps.

For four months now I have been regularly taking your basic formula *Vitacor Plus,* as well as *Arteriforte* and *Relacor.*

For the last two months my blood pressure has gone down from 180 / 110 to 145 / 80. In addition, the **dizzy spells** have disappeared completely and the headaches have also **drastically subsided.**

It was my son who drew my attention to your Cellular Medicine formulae, and I am so glad he did.

I would also like to recommend your vitamins to other people.

Yours sincerely,

Gerda Hunger

Dear Dr. Rath,

My wife, aged 38, has suffered from **bad migraine since she was a child.** The doctors simply did not know what to do, were unable to do anything more for her, and even wanted to admit her for psychiatric treatment. Fortunately, her mother was able to prevent that from happening.

Finally, my wife had to take **strong morphine-based painkillers,** and always had a supply of them in the fridge so she could be injected at short notice anytime night or day. The side effects meant that she was very restricted in her job (she is in nursing).

Acute circulatory problems and the related migraine attacks meant that she was often confined to **bed for days at a time**. All the medication she was taking managed to stop the attacks, but nothing that she tried brought her any fundamental help.

That is why I did not have any faith when she began your vitamin programme *(Vitacor Plus, Arteriforte, Metavicor)* at the beginning of June this year; I just thought it would be another useless and expensive attempt at combating the illness.

After just three months I was shown to be quite wrong. As early as the beginning of August she was feeling much better. Today, my wife is able to do without **some of her strong medication, and she has had no more migraine attacks.** Thank you very much!

Yours sincerely,

Mathias Dörfer

Dear Dr. Rath,

I am 38 years of age and used to be prone to migraine. After about June 1996 the **migraine attacks** increased in severity so that I sometimes suffered from nausea.

At the beginning of April 1997 I also started to suffer from circulation problems in the upper left half of my head. These caused me to have **difficulties with my balance,** so bad that I no longer dared to walk anywhere for fear I might fall over. The ears, nose and throat specialist prescribed me infusions and I took Dusodril tablets for one year.

At the beginning of this year, in February, I happened by chance to hear about Dr. Rath. Since the beginning of March I have been taking *Vitacor Plus* regularly - just one tablet to start with, and then since the beginning of July two a day.

My migraine has disappeared completely. This is absolutely wonderful. I have also had no more **circulation problems and dizzy spells!** My parents, my wife, my sister and my friend have also been taking the tablets for a while now, and they are very happy.

Yours respectfully,

P. L.

Dear Dr. Rath,

I am 35 years old and have been suffering **from bad headaches** for ten years. I would particularly suffer from them in stress situations and if I was not getting enough sleep. The pains were really awful.

In March this year I began taking one tablet of your basic formula *Vitacor Plus* three times a day.

Eight weeks later my headaches had left me completely. After a long day at work I am no longer as tense as I used to be.

I am so grateful that I found out about your vitamin programme, that I am able to use it, and that it has done me good.

Yours sincerely,

Kerstin Mende

Vitacor Plus™

The basic vitamin program for everyone, young and old alike!

3 tablets contain:

Vitamin C from:	
Ascorbic Acid	230 mg
Ascorbyl Palmitate	170 mg
Calcium Ascorbate	100 mg
Magnesium Ascorbate	100 mg
Vitamin E (d-Alpha-Tocopherol)	130 IU
Vitamin A (Beta-Carotene)	1665 IU
Vitamin B1 (Thiamine)	7 mg
Vitamin B2 (Riboflavine)	7 mg
Vitamin B3 from:	
Niacin	10 mg
Niacinamide	35 mg
Pantothenic Acid (d-Calcium Pantothenate)	40 mg
Vitamin B6 (Pyridoxal Phosphate)	10 mg
Vitamin B12 (Cyanocobalamine)	20 µg
Vitamin D3 (Cholecalciferol)	130 IU
Folic Acid	90 µg
Biotin	65 µg
L-Proline	110 mg
L-Lysine	110 mg
L-Carnitine	35 mg
L-Arginine	40 mg
L-Cysteine	35 mg
Calcium (Glycinate)	35 mg
Magnesium (Glycinate)	40 mg
Potassium (Chelate)	20 mg
Zinc (Glycinate)	7 mg
Manganese (Chelate)	1.3 mg
Copper (Glycinate)	330 µg
Selenium (L-Seleno Methionine)	20 µg
Chromium (Glycinate)	10 µg
Molybdenum (Glycinate)	4 µg
Inositol	35 mg
Coenzyme Q10	7 mg
Phosphorus (Dicalcium Phosphate)	15 mg
Pycnogenol™	7 mg
Citrus Bioflavonoids	100 mg

Additional natural vitamin E	**22 mg**
(Beta, Gamma and Delta Tocopherol)	
Additional natural Carotinoids	**50 µg**
(Alpha-Carotene, Lutein, Zea- and Cryptoxanthin)	

Additional information is available from the person who gave you this health brochure.

Arteriforte ™

A deficiency of vitamin C and other essential nutrients in the blood vessel wall is the primary cause of blood vessel dysfunction, causing:

- instability of the arterial wall
- cracks in the interior vessel wall
- formation of atherosclerotic deposits
- heart attack, stroke
- circulatory problems

Natural prevention and correction:

Optimum stability and elasticity of the artery walls is achieved through optimum production of collagen, elastin and other structural components of the blood vessel wall. The following nutrients support vascular cells in this function:

- **Vitamin C**
- **Chondroitin Sulfate**
- **N-Acetylglucosamine**
- **Lysine**
- **Proline**

In addition, antioxidant protection of the vascular cell membranes ensures optimum function of cells of the cardiovascular system. The most effective antioxidants are:

- **Vitamin E**
- **Vitamin C**

Cellular Medicine Formulas ™

Diacor™

The primary cause of cardiovascular problems in diabetes is a deficiency of vitamins and other essential nutrients in the cells of the body.

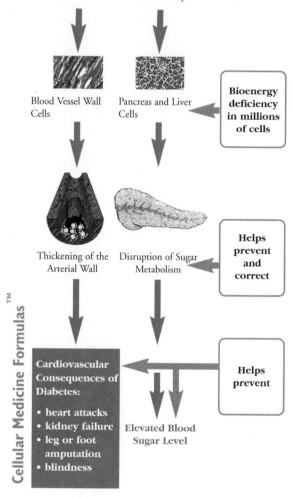

Blood Vessel Wall Cells

Pancreas and Liver Cells

Bioenergy deficiency in millions of cells

Thickening of the Arterial Wall

Disruption of Sugar Metabolism

Helps prevent and correct

Cellular Medicine Formulas™

Cardiovascular Consequences of Diabetes:

- heart attacks
- kidney failure
- leg or foot amputation
- blindness

Elevated Blood Sugar Level

Helps prevent

Enercor™

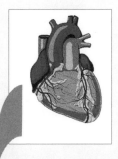

Chronic deficiency of vitamins and other cell bio-energy factors is the most frequent cause of low energy production in the heart muscle. Insufficient bioenergy in millions of heart muscle cells weakens the heart pumping action, reducing blood circulation in the body, manifested as shortness of breath, edema, and lack of energy.

Balanced vitamin and mineral complex in the Enercor™ nutritional supplement program provides nutrients supporting cellular bioenergy production in the heart muscle, thus improving the pumping performance of the heart.

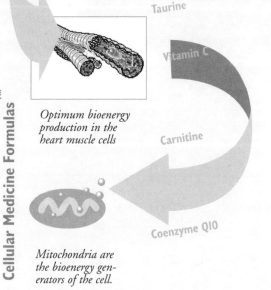

Cellular Medicine Formulas™

Taurine

Vitamin C

Carnitine

Coenzyme Q10

Optimum bioenergy production in the heart muscle cells

Mitochondria are the bioenergy generators of the cell.

Femicell^{TM}

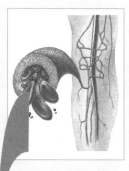

Women of childbearing age regularly lose blood during the monthly cycle and with the blood, the essential nutrients, which are needed for the building and maintenance of an efficient oxygen transport, defeating infections, optimum blood clotting ability, and other functions.

The consequences are anemia, frequent fatigue, susceptibility to infections and low vitality of the body.

The optimal intake of the most important nutrients contributes to optimum blood formation and thus prevents deficiency symptoms and diseases.

Cellular Medicine Formulas^{TM}

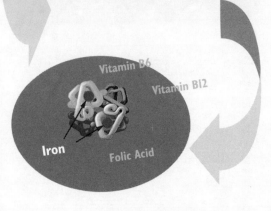

Vitamin B6

Vitamin B12

Iron

Folic Acid

Femiforte™

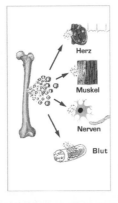

Hormonal changes associated with menopause also affect the female body is require for essential nutrients. The intake of calcium and magnesium and of trace elements, such as boron, is particularly important. These nutrients are needed for preventing the loss of bone tissue (osteoporosis). If they are not obtained from the diet or from dietary supplements, then the body will mobilize these minerals from their reservoir in the bones in order to maintain essential body functions, such as contraction of the muscle and the nervous system functions.

Natural ways to healthy bones and skeletal system

- optimum intake of bone-forming nutrients such as calcium, vitamin D, boron, and other minerals and trace elements.

- regular physical activity.

Cellular Medicine Formulas™

Balanced distribution and incorporation of minerals into the collagen network of the bone, supported by vitamin C, is the prerequisite for strong, hard bones and the prevention of osteoporosis.

Metavicor™

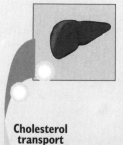

Most of the cholesterol in our body does not originate from the diet, but rather it is produced in the liver according to body needs. The main reason for an elevated production of cholesterol and other risk factors is a deficiency of vitamins and other essential nutrients.

Cholesterol transport

B-vitamins and also vitamin C, regulate the production and metabolism of cholesterol in our body.

Vitamin E

Vitamin C

Vitamin E and vitamin C protect cholesterol and other fat molecules from oxidation

Niacin (Vitamin B3)

Vitamin C

Carnitine

Cellular Medicine Formulas™

Relacor™

A deficiency of vitamins and other essential nutrients in millions of blood vessel wall cells is the most frequent cause of high blood pressure. These nutritional deficiencies can result in spasms and thickening of the artery wall, and can lead to elevated blood pressure increasing the risk of atherosclerosis and cardiovascular disease.

Natural prevention and correction:

Well-nourished cells in the vascular wall can optimally contract and relax, preventing vascular spasm and maintaining normal blood pressure.

Optimum distribution of minerals between inside and outside of vascular cells helps to rela the arterial wall.

Magnesium

Calcium

Cellular Medicine Formulas™

Arginine

The amino acid Arginine is a source of nitric oxide, a "relaxing factor" which helps in normalizing blood pressure in the cardiovascular system.

223

You can find further up-to-date information about vitamin research and Cellular Medicine in Dr. Rath's best seller "Why Animals Don't Have Heart Attacks - But People Do" as well as on the Internet.

Our Internet address www.rath.nl has become one of the world's most frequently consulted sources of information on natural health.

Every day thousands of people all over the world visit the site in their quest for essential information, information they can find nowhere else.